Win By
Not Losing

Win By Not Losing

A Disciplined Approach to Building and Protecting Your Wealth in the Stock Market by Managing Your Risk

NICHOLAS ATKESON
ANDREW HOUGHTON

New York   Chicago   San Francisco   Athens   London
Madrid   Mexico City   Milan   New Delhi
Singapore   Sydney   Toronto

1 2 3 4 5 6 7 8 9 0   DOC/DOC   1 9 8 7 6 5 4 3

ISBN   978-0-07-181290-0
MHID   0-07-181290-3

e-ISBN   978-0-07-181291-7
e-MHID   0-07-181291-1

This publication is designed to provide accurate and authoritative information in regard to the subject matter covered. It is sold with the understanding that neither the author nor the publisher is engaged in rendering legal, accounting, securities trading, or other professional services. If legal advice or other expert assistance is required, the services of a competent professional person should be sought.

> —*From a Declaration of Principles Jointly Adopted by a Committee of the American Bar Association and a Committee of Publishers and Associations*

Library of Congress Cataloging-in-Publication Data

Atkeson, Nicholas.
  Win by not losing: a disciplined approach to building and protecting your wealth in the stock market by managing your risk / by Nicholas Atkeson and Andrew Houghton.
    pages cm
  Includes bibliographical references.
  ISBN-13: 978-0-07-181290-0 (alk. paper)
  ISBN-10: 0-07-181290-3 (alk. paper)
  1. Stocks.   2. Investments.   3. Portfolio management.   I. Houghton, Andrew.
II. Title.
  HG4661.A885 2013
  332.63'22—dc23   2013013989

To Shawn for his incredible generosity and
support over the years
and
To C.J. for hiring us as stock jocks

Contents

Foreword

A S COFOUNDER and chairman emeritus of the MoneyShow, the largest self-directed investor conference series in the world, I have spent the past 35 years helping individual investors find winning investment strategies. During these four decades, I have often been frustrated that the retail investment industry for the most part has provided cookie-cutter-type advice involving allocating your hard-won savings into standardized mass-market investment products that are ill suited to handle rapidly changing market conditions.

Unfortunately, many of you have been poorly served by your financial advisors. There is an awakening going on caused by the lack of stock market appreciation over the last 12 years and the shock of a more than 50 percent stock market crash in 2007–2009. Your retirement savings, your children's education funds, and your overall wealth have not advanced in more than a decade. Something is wrong. What financial advisors have been preaching is not working.

It turns out that what seems wrong is actually quite normal when you look at long-term stock market "supercycles." Over the last 112 years of the Dow Jones Industrial Average, there have been four periods of 17 to 25 years in which the market has shown no meaningful appreciation and experienced high volatility.

When I first met Nick and Andrew, they were speakers on a panel discussion, talking about asset allocation in the new investment environment at the World MoneyShow in Orlando. I have moderated hundreds of these panel discussions, and virtually all the advice provided to investors comes down to grin and bear it during the hard times in the stock market. When I heard stock managers Nick and

Andrew say without hesitation that there are times when you should not own any stocks, I nearly fell out of my chair. Finally, someone was stating the obvious. Here were advisors focused not just on fee collection but on absolute returns. I could not wait to hear what they had to say next.

What Nick and Andrew show you in this book is how to take a completely different approach to investing. They show you how to look at the investment world from the standpoint of "how much money might I lose?" rather than "how much money might I make?" By protecting your capital first, you will learn how to make a fortune. Chasing return often leads to the poorhouse, whereas protecting capital is Warren Buffett's first and second rule of investing.

They explain the importance of evaluating and measuring risk when investing. Risk, rather than return, is the important metric. The first reason why risk is so important is basic math. Positive and negative returns are not symmetric. If you lose 50 percent of your portfolio, you have to have appreciation of 100 percent to get back to breakeven. Too many of us are spending the bulk of our investment years just trying to get back to where we were years ago.

Second, changes in perceptions of risk are an important driver of stock prices in the short and intermediate term rather than expected return (company earnings). Although earnings move up and down, they hardly budge relative to the radical short-term movements in perceived risk. In 2008, the CBOE market volatility index (VIX)—considered a measure of perceived market risk—jumped from the midteens to 89.53, a climb of almost 500 percent in a few months. The jump in risk perceptions during the late summer of 2008 gave us the worst market collapse since the Great Depression. Rising risk perceptions are horrible for markets if you are looking for appreciation. Falling risk perceptions make for bullish markets.

The purpose of this book is to (1) teach you what market metrics are really important when it comes to building wealth, (2) give you the tools to measure these important metrics, and (3) provide you with a disciplined system for knowing when to buy, what to buy, and when to sell. In short, Nick and Andrew take the myth and emotion out of investing and replace it with a proven, disciplined method of building and protecting wealth.

This book provides you with the tools to actively manage your portfolio in a nontrending market and, for that matter, any market. Unlike the famous manager of the Fidelity Magellan Fund, Peter Lynch, who talks about "investing in what you know," this book is much more focused on when you invest than on what you invest in when it comes to stocks. It is not necessary to be an expert in a company to find winning stocks. The market will let you know who the winners are. All you have to do is know when to own them and, most important, when to sell them.

Benjamin Graham's book *Security Analysis* on value investing is in its fourth edition. Once again, value investing requires the investor to perform a significant amount of research into individual companies that may not offer a real edge in today's information economy and high-frequency computer-controlled trading and index-fund-driven stock market. The focus of this book is not on individual companies but on stocks in the aggregate. Although a company may be great, it may simultaneously be a lousy stock. Much more important than the action of a single stock is the action of the overall market. When you are investing, you want the wind at your back. You are much more likely to own a winning stock if the market is moving higher in the aggregate than you are if the market is depreciating.

If Nick and Andrew were talking only about the theory of investing, their message would not have much impact. What really jumps out is that they are speaking from the experience of having created long-term, audited real-world results. After you read this book, your approach to investing will be changed forever. If you are looking for straightforward, actionable guidance on how to stay out of major down markets and participate in major up markets, you have found the right book.

Mark Twain once wrote, "October. This is one of the peculiarly dangerous months to speculate in stocks. The others are July, January,

September, April, November, May, March, June, December, August, and February." Your investment success depends on migrating your investment approach away from buy and hope to a proactive program of staying out of major down markets and participating in major up markets.

CHARLES GITHLER

Our Offer to You

THANK YOU for buying *Win By Not Losing*. The entire point of this book is to give you actionable advice with which to build and protect wealth. We go all the way from describing a concept to giving you the tools with which to make money.

What this book will show you is that diversification in a stock portfolio helps protect an investor only from stock-specific risk. It does nothing to protect an investor from a major market drop. The reason you have been told to stay in the market is that (1) you don't want to miss the times of appreciation, (2) you do not know when they will occur, and (3) if you stay invested over the long term, the market always goes higher. The truth is that (1) missing the major down periods is much more important for investment returns than is capturing the major up periods and (2) the market moves in supercycles in which for long periods it trends sideways to down and, from the standpoint of your personal investment horizon, does not always trend higher. The book concludes with specific methods for staying out of major down markets.

Books are static. Once a book is written, it does not update itself. To make the concepts in this book truly effective on an ongoing basis, we will need a way to stay in touch.

Because you have purchased this book, our offer to you is that we will waive the fees for a six-month subscription to our newsletter, *The Delta Wealth Accelerator*. If you read this book and combine it with the updated information from *The Delta Wealth Accelerator*, you will be well on your way to staying out of major down markets and participating in major up markets. You will finally be on your way to a prosperous and robust wealth accumulation program.

To sign up for your free six-month subscription to *The Delta Wealth Accelerator* newsletter, go to www.deltawealthaccelerator.com

and enter your name, e-mail address, and zip code. You can always reach us at www.deltaim.com. From the Internet, we can migrate the conversation to the phone or an in-person meeting. We invite you to read the book, check out the newsletter, and then talk with us about any questions you may have or how the concepts presented might best apply to your financial considerations.

The Delta Wealth Accelerator. *The Delta Wealth Accelerator* offers investors a simple-to-follow proven method by which to dynamically allocate assets to consistently make money. Learn how to participate in bullish market cycles and avoid major bearish markets. *The Delta Wealth Accelerator* would have helped you sidestep the 2001 crash and kept you out of the equity market before the collapse in the second half of 2008.

The Delta Wealth Accelerator does not rely on sophisticated strategies such as short selling and options trading. Unlike hedge funds, *The Delta Wealth Accelerator* shrewdly negotiates the market by using the best of today's low-cost trading instruments. Investment recommendations may include stocks, exchange-traded funds (ETFs), and mutual funds. The variety of instruments allows investors to control trading costs and stay involved with trades with which they are comfortable.

This newsletter service will provide you with the following:

1. A market landscape that lays out the current investment opportunities and challenges
2. Specific market timing signals
3. Actionable trade recommendations: when to buy, what to buy, and when to sell
4. Ways to avoid major down markets

Introduction

THE ECONOMIST John Kenneth Galbraith once said, "The conventional view serves to protect us from the painful job of thinking." Who has the time to stop and question the conventional view as long as it is working? It is during times when the conventional view no longer offers a good explanation of reality that new thinking is required.

My (Nick's) youngest daughter was born in 1998. As diligent, responsible parents, we began saving for her college education during her first year and have continued doing that every year since then. When we made the first contribution to her college fund in November 1999, the S&P 500 Index was at roughly 1,389. After roughly 13 years, the S&P 500 was at 1,330, down about 4 percent. Her initial account balance of $10,000 shrank to $9,575. Knowing that since 1900 the average annual return of the stock market (measured by the Dow Jones Industrial Average) was 9.4 percent, including dividends, did my daughter no good. Knowing that stocks have a higher level of average returns than do bonds over long periods added nothing to the account.

It turns out that this dismal stretch of market history is not unique. From 1965 through 1982, the stock market went nowhere and suffered from incredibly high levels of volatility, including a 66 percent high-to-low drop for the average stock in 1973 and 1974. The same thing happened from 1906 to 1924 (18 years) and from 1928 to 1953 (25 years). During these periods, stocks showed almost no cumulative appreciation.

Amazingly, despite the poor investment results of the last decade and a market history that strongly supports the thesis that buying and holding a broadly diversified fund is not an effective investment strategy during all market cycles, the retail investment industry has made almost no perceptible effort to change its recommended investment programs to match the current market environment and your investment needs.

Equity investment choices are almost all buy-and-hold-style funds. If you are fortunate enough to have a personal financial advisor, you generally pay a high fee for the advisor to hold your hand while you suffer through whatever the market can throw at you in what boils down to just another buy-and-hold program.

Buy and hold has been the conventional view. As long as it worked during the 1982–2000 bull market, there was little motivation to question it. Buy and hold during an 18-year bull market cycle was easy and tax-efficient and delivered better returns than many active managers could. Over a decade after the end of the great bull market, investors are beginning the painful process of rethinking how they should invest. As we look over the long history of the market, it is evident that the market tends to stair step higher with the bulk of the market action showing little sustained appreciation. The conventional view of buy and hold has not been an effective investment tactic during much of the market's history.

Our lives are playing out right now. We need our investments to keep pace. Based on when we were born and when our children were born, we can predict with a fair amount of certainty when we will need capital for education, homes, and retirement. We need a way to make our money work for us so that our life story can be as full as possible.

Andrew Houghton and I have had a front row seat in the investment products industry for the last 20 years. We have worked in the heart of the industry—the sell-side investment bank—selling institutional research, taking initial public offering (IPO) allocations, and helping shape the mutual funds that end up in your account. Not only do we know the research process that is used to influence which equities are hot and which are not at a nuts-and-bolts level from the ground up, we know the people and processes on the mutual and hedge fund side equally well.

We both started work on the institutional sales desk of Montgomery Securities, which means we sold proprietary stock research to mutual funds and hedge funds. Montgomery was a small investment bank specializing in funding the growth of companies predominantly in the technology, healthcare, and consumer discretionary sectors. Microsoft (MSFT) went public in 1986. Cisco Systems (CSCO) went public in 1992. By the late 1990s, the power of funding growth companies was fully evident as the tech bubble raged and the Nasdaq approached 5,000; Montgomery was involved in an IPO or secondary offering almost every other business day.

Montgomery Securities was acquired by NationsBank, which then acquired Bank of America and changed its name to Bank of America. We rode through these transitions, observing the operating differences of the small, entrepreneurial investment bank versus the Goliaths of the financial world.

Over the next decade, from 2000 to 2010, the sell-side institutional investment world was a stormy one. Technology obliterated trading margins. Trading floors filled with people gave way to computer trading platforms in which millions of shares transact without the aid of direct human intervention in programs called HFT (high-frequency trading). Sometimes the computers go haywire, creating episodes such as the May 6, 2010, Flash Crash, in which the Dow Jones Industrial Average fell 1,000 points, or 9 percent, in a matter of minutes. Derivatives trading became a tremendously powerful force, eventually helping push American capitalism to the brink of collapse in the 2007–2009 credit crisis. Several major firms (Bear Stearns, Lehman Brothers, Wachovia, Merrill Lynch, Fannie Mae, Freddie Mac, AIG—too many to be fully listed) failed or were consumed by stronger players.

Andrew and I passed through this era on the strength of our trust-based institutional relationships. No matter what the game or the technology, we maintained our standards and won business on the basis of substance and putting the client first. We migrated into the world's largest options trading firm, Susquehanna, in 2003. We helped Susquehanna expand its reach into the deepest and richest parts of the institutional world with its options intelligence and specialized research products. We saw how exchange-traded funds (ETFs) are built, managed, and traded by the pros. We discovered the important information flows embedded in options trading and learned how to tease out important market intelligence. We learned about cross-asset class information transfer at Susquehanna, which allowed us to take our next step in an industry undergoing radical change.

From Susquehanna, we launched a black box quantitative hedge fund, trading stocks on the basis of information found in institutional options trades. We learned that for the right institutional clients, it was possible to bypass the standard rules of leverage and leverage one's trading activities up to 10:1. This type of excessive risk taking was encouraged as it meant more fee income to the investment banks. While we turned down offers of excessive leverage, we gained extensive firsthand knowledge of trading huge blocks of securities in automated, computerized trading programs with the push of a button. On the days when the market does something that is explained as a "fat finger" problem, it is quite possible that this is the case. We have seen it firsthand.

During our years in some of the most sophisticated and largest institutional investment firms, it was clear that the basic investment needs of the average investor were not being addressed adequately. It may not come as a surprise to you that the financial world is run by and for major institutional firms. Their business is to maximize profits over relatively short periods. Sometimes short-term profit maximization comes at the cost of long-term viability. As we have seen from the recent taxpayer-supported bailouts, major financial institutions and the common person are often not working toward a common goal.

We know that what is being delivered to you is not the answer. The vast majority of investment products do little to respond to your investment objectives and investment time frame. When regular folks ask what they should do with their money, there are few good answers. Most people do not have access to hedge funds or special private equity deals. They cannot invest the way the Harvard, Stanford, and Yale endowments do, with 30 to 40 percent of their portfolios being placed in well-vetted alternative funds.

In this book we show you how to move from passive investing to proactive investing much the way some of the more successful institutions invest their own money. We show you how to use a time-tested, disciplined, and tactical approach to investing in equities.

The investment lessons in this book are crucial to you if you want to build and protect wealth over time. Without the disciplined investment process described in this book, you are at the mercy of the market and your investment tools will be crude instruments.

The first principle of making money is learning how not to lose it. This is a book about making money, which means we will first show you how to avoid losing it. This book is not intended to be an academic discussion of economic theory. It is a practical guide, written by practitioners of the art, to building wealth by avoiding major down markets and participating in major up markets.

Authors' Note

WE HAVE tried to write a financial book that is readable, enjoyable, and usable. To do this, we have used the personal stories of a variety of investors to highlight important investment concepts. These stories are interesting and entertaining and should suffice on their own to make the investment principles clear. We also provide some of the financial theory that explains and supports the underlying investment ideas (Chapters 5 and 6). If you are reading the financial theory portion of this book and are getting bogged down, feel free to skip forward. The basic conclusions do not require that you be an economist or financial expert.

Win By
Not Losing

PART ONE

Streaks and Investing

CHAPTER ONE

The Story of Sonny

Some stories start with "I know a guy who knows a guy who knows a guy." In this case, we actually do know the guy. Not only do we know him, we sat next to him on a trading desk for years. The guy is named Sonny.

We start our story with Sonny because he rode one of the hottest of hot streaks that we are aware of. It was not like amassing a fortune on a single major idea like Bill Gates starting Microsoft or Mark Zuckerberg founding Facebook; it was a streak involving an amazing series of wins. It was a streak based on investment discipline in a part of the world in which the odds and expectations say you can't win.

Sonny was born in the city of San Francisco. He lived near Golden Gate Park. The park taught Sonny how to know a streak when he saw one and how to make the most of it.

In his early teens, Sonny spent a lot of time in the park. The park had 22 tennis courts and attracted many world-class tennis players. Guys would come from all over the world to play tennis there. Sonny spent a lot of time on those courts on his way to becoming a world-ranked tennis player.

Sonny was a self-made player. He honed his technical tennis skills by watching others play. Sonny's specialty was street ball; he could hook with the best of them. He played the mind game and never backed down when challenged. He was also physically gifted in a way that suited the demands of tennis well.

Within sight of the tennis courts were the old guys playing backgammon. Like the courts, the park attracted many outstanding backgammon players. Thus, in one spot, you had many of the world's best tennis and backgammon players. As a 13-year-old, Sonny could not resist the temptation to wander from the courts and into the world of backgammon. He would play backgammon for hours and hours against the older guys. At any one time, there would be six games going at once. Players would pair off according to ability and move up and down the line of boards on the basis of their winnings. Gambling was always part of the game and sharpened Sonny's concentration.

As good a tennis player as Sonny was, he became an even better backgammon player. Like all the best players, he knew exactly what to do on every single roll of the dice. Six hours a day of backgammon on the weekends and in the summers can do that to a person. The odds favored Sonny against anyone who did not understand the underlying probabilities and subtleties of the game perfectly. Sonny was a street-smart kid who was a natural when it came to intuitively understanding odds and risk management. Sonny's combination of a mathematical brain, street savvy, and not flinching or backing down when challenged emerged as a powerful combination of skills that served him well in larger venues such as Wall Street and Las Vegas.

Sonny began betting before investing. In sports, there was always gambling with Sonny. Betting on sports migrated into the more disciplined betting associated with world-class backgammon. Backgammon was interrupted by occasional trips to Reno and Tahoe. Everyone Sonny knew gambled. Although it might seem like a lot of money to most, Sonny felt he started small with an average bet at the blackjack table of about $500 to $1,000 per hand.

On one of Sonny's first trips to Las Vegas, he won 20 blackjack hands in a row. His average bet was $1,000. His winnings reached $20,000. He stopped. Sonny knew the odds were stacked against him in the casino. Without emotion, he understood that one of his few protections was to just stop playing. Rather than letting the excitement and emotions of a big win overwhelm his thinking, Sonny remained cool and firmly grounded in probabilistic math. Whereas

most first-time Vegas winners give it all back by feeling good and getting careless, Sonny just walked away. His early years playing some
of the best in backgammon, often with meaningful bets at stake,
prepared him for seeing this streak as just another day at the office.

Sonny came to Wall Street during the time of Michael Milken's
fall from grace and the junk bond market collapse in the late 1980s.
Government-backed bonds, including municipal bonds, were selling
for pennies on the dollar. Sonny's firm would put a sizable markup
on the bonds and sell them to individual investors. Whereas Sonny's
profit from the markup was significant, his client base made out like
bandits as almost all the distressed bonds purchased ended up paying
out at 100 cents on the dollar.

Two years later, Sonny was sitting on the trading desk of one of
the fastest-growing investment banks in the world, selling growth
stocks to investors during one of the greatest boom cycles ever experienced in the financial markets. His clients loved him for his tenacity
in protecting their interests on trade executions and deal allocations.
From a base of $40,000 per year, Sonny was soon taking home seven
figures and enjoying a hot streak of epic proportions.

While the stock market raged, Sonny found time to continue his
regular trips to Las Vegas. His average hand had grown from roughly
$1,000 to $50,000. Yellow chips ($1,000) were being replaced with
brown ($5,000), orange ($25,000), and white chips ($100,000). With
one, two, or three hands of blackjack going simultaneously, Sonny
would play an average of 400 hands per hour, seven times the amount
of most Vegas gamblers. At $50,000 per hand and 400 hands per
hour, Sonny was moving roughly $20 million an hour.

With splits and doubles, Sonny would have as much as $300,000
out on the table on a single hand. Having been tempered by years of
making calculated bets, Sonny did not flinch or change his discipline
when the stakes became stratospheric. No matter how high the stakes
went, Sonny kept his emotions out of the equation.

Casinos would spend as much as $200,000 to have Sonny visit.
Private jets, including Boeing 727s with gold-plated everything, were
sent to bring Sonny to the casino with a group of his friends. Sonny's

hotel room would often be 10,000 square feet with a private pool and golf area, about five times larger than the average American detached home. A few hours with Sonny at the poolside cabana could cost the casino $15,000.

One evening, while visiting Sonny in a Vegas casino that subsequently shut down its "whale" gambling group because of him, we asked Sonny if he could think of anything the casino would not provide him if he asked. After careful consideration, Sonny said no. Private jet flights to Paris, three personal assistants, any amount of extravagant gifts, and so on, made it clear that the casinos meant business.

In 2001, Super Bowl XXXV was held in Tampa, Florida. A casino called Sonny and said it would send Hall of Fame quarterbacks John Elway and Jim Kelly out to his house to pick him up in a limo and escort him to the game in a private jet. Sonny's tickets were in the same section as the players' families, and he would be brought to the game from his hotel with a police escort surrounding his limo. Sonny told the casino to send the jet but said he would replace the quarterbacks with eight of his friends and he wanted to stop in New Orleans on the way out.

In New Orleans, Sonny was the show. The casino was not used to dealing with $50,000 hands and had only $100 chips readily available. The dealer was so nervous that he could not stop shaking and sweating. As usual, Sonny was moving fast, and the dealer was really struggling with the math of managing so many chips. On one hand, the dealer made a $60,000 payout mistake in Sonny's favor. Sonny ended up winning $260,000. He then placed bets on the Super Bowl coin toss and winner for good measure. Needless to say, Sonny won the flip and the Ravens paid out nicely.

Although the gifts and privileges extended to Sonny may seem extravagant, they are part of a calculated bet. Casinos have what is known as a "theoretical," or "Theo," that they apply to their high-roller customers. It is the theoretical win percentage formula the casino uses to calculate what its win percentage should be over time. Essentially, the Theo is a calculation of the expected profits to the casino by multiplying the player's time played by the dollar amount played by the winning percentage. Every hand played by Sonny is tracked by the casino. They could tell him exactly what cards were played and how he bet through his entire history with the casino. Solely on the basis of the numbers, Sonny looked like a good customer.

Although a casino has the underlying odds of blackjack on its side, it attempts to tilt the game further in its favor by bringing emotions to the forefront. Players who fly in private jets, stay in big hotel rooms, and are treated like royalty often become addicted to the lifestyle. They can't stop because they want the gratification of the special attention. Time is working against them. They are no longer the disciplined gamblers they once were but addicts to the high life. These players also can feel indebted in a subtle way to the casino. Losing becomes not a loss but just an indirect way of paying for the lifestyle. Casinos will do all they can to make gamblers feel bad about losing. The emotional reaction can make gamblers not want to walk away until they are winners again. Once again, the casino has extended the time of play and the probability of capturing its Theo.

Sonny never forgot who he was and where he came from. Before going to Las Vegas, he would spend up to two days making sure that the game was arranged in accordance with his rules. Sonny does not gamble unless the game meets his rules. Big-time gamblers negotiate a "discount" on lost dollars. In this case, Sonny would not play the game unless the discount was set at a minimum of at least 25 percent. In other words, if Sonny lost $100,000, the real loss was reduced by 25 percent to $75,000. Sonny would play on the "rim." A rim is essentially a line of credit. The difference between playing on the rim and taking a mark is that rim credit does not slow the speed of play. When Sonny hits a streak, the first thing the casino wants to do is slow the speed of or even stop play. On the rim, this is not possible.

The other aspect of playing on the rim is that it makes the credit drawdown highly visible. Two pit bosses stand behind the dealer and make sure that the accounting of the credit line that is shown on the table is kept current. For Sonny, this forces a certain discipline by which he never confuses the money stack as his until the rim is paid off. In any event, Sonny sets his loss limits well before the game begins. He walks away when his preordained loss limit is reached without exception.

In addition to setting the discount and establishing the rim, Sonny would often require that the casino provide him with two dedicated tables. At this level of blackjack, no other gamblers are at Sonny's tables and usually no other gamblers are in the room. It is somewhat akin to an old-style western gunfight in which the street is cleared and the two gunfighters square off at 20 paces. In this case, the stage is cleared for the casino and Sonny to go at it one on one. When we watched this first hand, our palms were sweaty and it was mind-blowing how fast the money and chips were moving. His ability to stay disciplined and nonemotional seemed almost inhuman.

The lengthy preparation did not affect Sonny's playing discipline and his ability to quit the game when he was ahead. During one visit, he played for eight minutes and walked away with roughly three times the annual income of the average annual American household. The casino spent the money to bring Sonny and his entourage to Vegas, prepare the gaming room in accordance with Sonny's require-ments, pay the staff, and take care of Sonny for the remainder of the weekend. Sonny's group arrived in Vegas fresh with excitement for the big game. With eight minutes of elapsed time from start to end, the crowd clearly felt let down. None of this affected Sonny's disci-pline. He achieved his win target and quit on the win. Done. Eight minutes. Money in the bank.

When the casino later attempted to have Sonny pay for some of the expenses of his trip, including the $15,000 poolside cabana bill, he flatly refused. Sonny and the casino both understood the Theo and both knew that Sonny's primary safety mechanism was to stop playing. Sonny never lost sight of the math behind the game.

Sonny has won millions in Vegas over two decades. He has been one of the largest successful gamblers in the world. On one trip, Sonny tipped his casino host a house. Only two casinos have any current interest in having Sonny play. The only reason those casinos invite Sonny back is that there is high management turnover in these publicly traded companies and every new manager makes the same mistake of looking at Sonny's Theo and thinking this will be the time that he gives it back.

Sonny's secret is streaks and discipline. He plays high-velocity blackjack because the streaks occur at a higher frequency than they do in games such as poker and craps. Sonny would prefer not to wait too long for the next streak.

Before the streak comes, Sonny is patient. When the streak comes, he ramps up his investment exposure fast. As soon as the streak starts to end, Sonny walks away. He is not worried about walking away in six minutes if the streak comes fast. The time of play is inconsequential. As the winnings accumulate, he will often require the casino to cash him out. Once he is cashed out, the casino house rules do not allow Sonny to recash the check. If his money is in chips, he will often place the chips in a remote safe. Sonny does this to make sure that he avoids a major loss.

Sonny is not trying to win every penny. It is impossible to know if a streak has begun until it has shown some momentum and impossible to know it has ended until losses occur. Somewhat as in the stock market, he is not trying to bottom- or top-tick the trend; rather, he is trying to catch the bulk of the up move while avoiding most of the down move. As a whale customer in the casino playing his own tables, Sonny can ask the dealer to reshuffle the cards at any time as a way to interrupt downward momentum and can speed play and increase the size of the hands on upward momentum.

Having seen 20 winning hands in a row at the blackjack table, Sonny knows that streaks can have a powerful compounding effect on wealth. At $50,000 per hand, Sonny works with enough money to make the positive effects of catching a winning streak last. He knows that it is critical to bet enough to make a difference.

It is not about luck with Sonny. He spent years working in probabilistic betting environments with steadily increasing stakes to develop a keen sense for streaks and how to use a disciplined approach to capitalize on them. No matter what emotional temptations are presented to Sonny, he does not stray from his discipline. The few times Sonny did stray served as an expensive reminder to stick to his plan. Sonny only plays games that he knows inside and out and in which the rules are set the way he likes them. He does not play where he is unfamiliar and the risks are not known. Sonny is acutely concerned with not giving the money back and avoiding the big loss. He uses a variety of risk control measures, including walking away at any time to make sure he remains on the plus side. He is willing to be patient and wait for a positive streak to emerge before betting big. A series of small losses are made irrelevant by a string of large winning bets. It is not about the frequency of wins but about the magnitude.

Although the odds say the casinos should be more than happy to welcome whale business, many of the major casinos are moving away from this part of the market. The margins are too thin. By bringing in lots of average gamblers who make small bets, a casino expects to achieve a 20 percent profit margin. They have yet to make money on Sonny after 22 years. What is scary is that Sonny believes he is becoming more disciplined and efficient with time.

The reason why we started this book with the story of Sonny is that his experience and discipline go a long way toward explaining his "luck." Sonny's approach to blackjack holds important lessons for successful stock market investing. Know the game you are joining. Play the game according to your terms. Set out your plan before you play and stick to it. Be patient and wait for the right times to make your money. Do not worry about small losses as you wait to capture big wins. When a trend comes, recognize it and invest enough to make a material difference in your overall portfolio. When the trend fades, stop investing. Do not hesitate to walk away when the market is not conducive to making money. Have a plan for holding on to your winnings. Keep your emotions out of the investment process.

Win By Not Losing is all about building wealth and protecting capital.

Sonny's Takeaways

We do not advocate that you take up gambling in a casino as a way to invest, but Sonny's methods helped him win in an environment that is considerably more harsh to traders than is the U.S. stock market. You will see almost all of Sonny's methods repeated in the stories that follow. As this book progresses, the stories become increasingly focused on the stock market with higher levels of resolution on exactly what traders are thinking and doing when it comes to making money with streaks.

The recurring themes that are important to remember from Sonny's story are the following:

- Establish your trading rules in advance. Enter the game with a plan.
- Your plan should be based on real-world experience and have demonstrated positive results through a wide array of conditions.
- Be disciplined and stay with the plan. Keep your emotions out of it. Sonny's stare-down, high-stakes gambling is an incredible test of his ability to keep his emotions in check.
- Your best protection is to exit the game. When the streak runs against you, stop playing. There is no requirement to play every hand.
- It is always possible to have a situation that will break down any and all investment plans. Do not forget that these "black swan" events may occur and be ready to exit the game before the losses go beyond what is manageable.
- When you are on a positive streak, press the bet. In Sonny's case, he played the splits and doubles and increased the number of hands played as the positive streak progressed.
- Do not focus on catching the bullish or bearish streak on the first tick. In stock market terms, there is no need to buy at the absolute bottom and sell at the absolute top to be a winner. Focus on catching the bulk of the bullish streak an the bulk of the bearish streak. It takes a few hands that a bullish streak has begun or ended. Although

counterintuitive, your risk is reduced if you wait to make sure a streak has begun rather than being the first in or out. Moving too fast can create the risk of the "head fake," in which you are whipsawed in and out.

- Stay grounded. If you are fortunate and have major financial gains, do not forget your discipline. The game has not changed, and neither should you.

CHAPTER TWO

The Nature of Streaks

S CIENCE SAYS streaks are often explained by randomness. According to a variety of studies, including examinations of basketball shooting and baseball hitting streaks, statisticians posit that the streaks mostly happen without the benefit of our actions. If you are the beneficiary of a series of fortunate events, many analysts who view the world with a probabilistic model would say that is just good luck. Those who attempt to explain streaks as not being random are merely showing how our narrative-hungry brains can find patterns after the fact. The soft sciences make a strong effort, using math borrowed from the hard sciences, to say the world is mostly a random place.

This presents us with a huge opportunity. It opens the door to doing something that many investors have given up on: beating average market returns consistently over time with lower risk. Because most retail money is managed in a buy-and-hold manner in which fate determines the outcome, we have plenty of room to take the other side of the trade.

A streak is a run of similar outcomes. If streaks, especially in areas where money can be invested, are controllable and/or predictable events, this clearly has important investment implications.

In many cases when randomness is asserted as the best fit for the data, some basic fundamental issues are not being accounted for. For example, large waves tend to arrive at the beach in sets. You could say that wave patterns are random. However, you could also say the wind blows in gusts and that wind energy is a variable force that creates either large or small wave sets. The fetch (the distance of water available for wind to be transferred into wave energy) and the topography of the ocean floor are also factors. When you conduct a thorough analysis of wave patterns, you quickly discover that what may seem to be a random pattern actually is somewhat predictable with careful measurement of the input factors.

Surfers understand the streaky nature of waves. They lie on their boards and wait for a good wave set to roll in. When the set rolls in, they become hyperactive in their efforts to catch the best waves in the set. Surfers use their understanding of streaks to expend their energy riding the best waves and conserve their strength during times when the ocean is unlikely to yield a good ride. Today, surfers can use technology (buoy data) to know days in advance when the surf is likely to be good, much the way we use indicators to understand market patterns.

Academic studies will tell you that future stock prices are random events. As a result, many financial advisors and investors have become brainwashed into thinking that the stock market is essentially equally attractive at all times. The primary conclusion of this random thesis is to always be invested in the market. Using the surfer analogy, it would be like asking the surfer to always be in the water out of fear of missing the good waves. The problem with being in the water all the time is that the majority of time there are no waves to ride and you could be eaten by a shark.

We strongly believe not all streaks are random, particularly when it comes to investing. There are clearly times when investing in stocks (and options) is more likely to yield winners. In June 2008, we began writing an options investment newsletter. Over the next three months, we got on a hot streak. Volatility (options premium) exploded higher. We knew we were on a strong winning streak, and we made new trade recommendations at a rapid pace. Figure 2.1 shows a history of the first 33 trades we recommended to our subscribers.

Every trade recommendation is included in this list; we are not being selective. The basic point is that there are clearly good times to be an investor in equities (and derivatives of equities). We believe

Option	Date Opened	Entry Price	Date Closed	Closing Price	Return %	Position
CAVM Sept 20 Puts	6/4/2008	$1.00	7/22/2008	$4.10	310.00%	Long
CAVM Sept 20 Puts	6/4/2008	$1.00	7/9/2008	$4.20	320.00%	Long
CAVM Sept 20 Puts	6/4/2008	$1.00	7/8/2008	$2.70	170.00%	Long
UTSI July 5 Calls	6/5/2008	$0.60	7/9/2008	$0.60	0.00%	Long
UTSI July 5 Calls	6/5/2008	$0.60	6/18/2008	$0.90	50.00%	Long
BAC June 32.50 Calls	6/11/2008	$0.15	6/12/2008	$0.19	26.67%	Long
ORB Sept 25 Calls	6/12/2008	$1.40	8/20/2008	$1.55	10.71%	Long
ORB Sept 25 Calls	6/12/2008	$1.40	8/15/2008	$2.80	100.00%	Long
PMC Dec 20 Calls	6/13/2008	$3.00	9/4/2008	$4.60	53.33%	Long
WYNN Sept 95 Puts	6/19/2008	$10.00	9/10/2008	$14.10	41.00%	Long
WYNN Sept 95 Puts	6/19/2008	$10.00	7/10/2008	$21.50	115.00%	Long
LLL Aug 100 Calls	6/23/2008	$2.20	8/13/2008	$5.00	127.27%	Long
K Jan 40 Puts	6/23/2008	$0.70	7/15/2008	$0.65	-7.14%	Long
AER Oct 15 Calls	7/8/2008	$1.05	8/20/2008	$1.20	14.29%	Long
AER Oct 15 Calls	7/8/2008	$1.05	8/5/2008	$2.35	123.81%	Long
AER Oct 15 Calls	7/8/2008	$1.05	8/1/2008	$2.15	104.76%	Long
FRED Nov 15 Calls	7/25/2008	$0.75	9/3/2008	$0.75	0.00%	Long
FRED Nov 15 Calls	7/25/2008	$0.75	8/11/2008	$1.45	93.33%	Long
FDX Oct 75 Puts	7/31/2008	$3.70	10/8/2008	$5.70	54.05%	Long
DPS Feb 25 Calls	8/19/2008	$2.30	10/1/2008	$3.50	52.17%	Long
WERN March 22.50 Puts	8/20/2008	$2.80	10/3/2008	$4.25	51.79%	Long
BBT Oct 25 Puts	8/21/2008	$1.95	10/17/2008	$0.05	-97.44%	Long
CREE Sept 25 Calls	8/22/2008	$0.45	8/25/2008	$0.70	55.56%	Long
TRLG Oct 25 Puts	8/27/2008	$2.10	10/6/2008	$3.30	57.14%	Long
CLNE Oct 17.50 Calls	8/29/2008	$1.30	9/4/2008	$2.40	84.62%	Long
SNDA Oct 35 Calls	9/10/2008	$0.35	10/7/2008	$0.10	-71.43%	Long
SNDA Oct 35 Calls	9/10/2008	$0.35	9/24/2008	$0.65	85.71%	Long
AF Oct 20 Puts	9/10/2008	$0.95	9/18/2008	$2.10	121.05%	Long
OKS April 55 Calls	9/17/2008	$2.95	9/19/2008	$4.20	42.37%	Long
TIF Jan 40 Calls	9/24/2008	$3.00	9/25/2008	$3.10	3.33%	Long
SPG Jan 105 Calls	10/1/2008	$4.70	11/14/2008	$0.10	97.87%	Short
DOW Nov 22.50 Puts	10/23/2008	$1.10	11/4/2008	$0.25	77.27%	Short
ASML Dec 15 Puts	11/10/2008	$1.15	11/13/2008	$1.80	56.52%	Long

FIGURE 2.1   *Big Money Options* Newsletter: History of First 33 Trades

you can tilt the odds in your favor by investing during good times and staying out of the market during bad times. Because the odds of encountering a favorable versus a negative streak are predictable, you can make your own money-winning streaks and step out of the way when the odds of experiencing a winning streak are low.

Life has momentum. There are upward and downward spirals not only with individuals but also with companies and stocks. Microsoft (MSFT) won important initial contracts from IBM that enabled it to capture a nearly monopolistic position in the personal computing world as other firms embraced its operating system as the de facto industry standard. Out of a cluster of Internet search engines, Google (GOOG) achieved dominance as its browser became the browser of choice for several major consumer-facing technology platforms. One good contract often leads to another.

Alternatively, there are numerous examples in which poorly structured firms experience business contractions and the negative trends become much like dominoes falling in sequence. Nokia (NOK) was once the world's largest manufacturer of mobile phones. Then Apple (AAPL) persuaded consumers to carry a small computer in their pockets rather than a basic phone. Nokia's market share declined dramatically over several years. In October 2012, the company announced the sale of "non-core assets," including its headquarters building, in an effort to raise much-needed cash. Key personnel often leave faltering firms, and concerned customers migrate to other suppliers. The negative feedback loop gains momentum, and viability issues arise.

Probabilities can be conditional. Small advantages in life can translate into disproportionately large payoffs. Advantages and disadvantages can accrue to winners and losers, respectively.

Momentum is the product of mass and velocity. Downward markets tend to increase velocity as fear sparks emotional responses. Rising markets tend to attract increasing numbers of buyers. Recall how new investors scrambled to buy stocks during the dot-com bubble of the late 1990s. Almost everyone knows someone who considered abandoning a day job to become a stock trader. Stock tips abounded.

Compare that frenzied rush into stock investing with the disillusionment and lack of investor enthusiasm that occurred at the market bottom in March 2009. Less than a year and a half after touching 1,576.09, the S&P 500 traded as low as 666.79. For the next several years after the March 2009 market low, retail investors pulled their money out of equities at a record pace.

At the most basic level, the direction of stock market trading is often streaky because of the human emotions of fear and greed. Fear is a sensation that can be triggered rapidly and can overwhelm almost all other thoughts when it is fully turned on. It originates from deep within the medial temporal lobes of the brain complex in a part called the amygdala and is part of human survival hardwiring. When we get scared, we run. If we run fast enough, we live. If we live, we can make babies. With babies, the species lives to run again.

Fear is universal. When you are feeling maximum investment pain, so is the herd. If you are losing sleep over your stock investments, you can rest assured that thousands of other investors are doing exactly the same thing. You have been led to believe that the market is efficient, forward-looking, and rational. If stock values have been cut in half, it must necessarily mean that investors' expectations that a negative outcome will occur in the near future are true. Fear builds and spreads, and sellers overwhelm buyers until the sellers become exhausted. They have virtually nothing left to sell. Guess what? Right at the point of maximum pain and when even the strong hands have folded, the bottom has been marked. There are now more buyers than sellers, and the healing process begins. It is extremely rare for the negative expectations held by investors at a market bottom to play out in reality. Our fear often gets the better of us and causes us to be blind to potential positive outcomes and to exaggerate the negatives.

On October 19, 1987, the Dow Jones Industrial Average (DJIA) plunged 22.61 percent in a single day. After the crash, the *New York Times* ran a comparative chart of the market starting in 1929 and forecasting a multiyear market depression. In December 1987, 33 eminent economists from a variety of nations reacted to the difficult trading patterns of that year by predicting that "the next few years could be the most troubled since the 1930s." In less than two years from the December prediction by some of the most knowledgeable experts, the DJIA made a full recovery from the chaos and decline of October 1987. We recollect the period measured from 1982 through 1999 as being one of the best times to be a U.S. stock investor ever.

The emotion of greed can also have a powerful and predictable impact on security prices. When a stock starts to show positive momentum, investor greed is often stimulated. In recent market history, until the launch of iPhone 5 in November 2012, Apple (AAPL) was the hot stock. Investors bought the stock partly because its steady appreciation caused skepticism to be overpowered by greed. Because the stock market is rational, efficient, and forward-looking, it must necessarily be true and correct that the rise in a stock is fully justified by powerful fundamental forces. As has happened so many times before in a broad array of investments, Apple became an overcrowded trade that eventually ran into diminishing buying pressure. When the stock began to roll over in the first half of 2013, fear became rampant, and the stock lost roughly 45 percent of its value in five months.

For most of us, fear is a more powerful emotion than greed. Fear means you might survive, whereas greed leads to an accumulation of more things in your life that may or may not make you happier. Fear is primal, and greed is cerebral. As a result of the gentler influence of greed versus fear on our emotional state, markets tend to rise like a feather (bull markets tend to unfold over a period of years) and fall like an anvil: On October 19, 1987, the Dow Jones Industrial Average dropped 22.61 percent in a single day; in the May 6, 2010, Flash Crash, the DJIA dropped 1,000 points (9 percent) intraday; the Nasdaq was down roughly 80 percent in the dot-com bubble burst of 2000–2001; and the S&P 500 dropped from high to low by over 55 percent in the 2008–2009 credit crisis.

Fear breeds fear. Greed breeds greed. Fear is a more powerful emotion than greed. Fear and greed help shape and accentuate market trends.

A winning streak is often called good luck. But as we know, we can make our own luck. In 2002, the Oakland A's Major League Baseball team won 20 games in a row, the longest MLB winning streak since World War II. From a distance, an observer might have concluded that the streak was random and should be thought of as good luck. Upon closer inspection, the Oakland A's made their own luck. The A's tilted the odds in their favor by ignoring conventional baseball wisdom tied to traditional player scouting reports and relying instead on a systematic, quantitative analysis of collective player output to assemble a team optimized by a computer to win a target number of games. Team general manager Billy Beane upended decades of entrenched beliefs held by the baseball experts with his nonemotional and quantitative approach to finding the best players for the money.

Darrell Green, a cornerback with the Washington Redskins from 1983 to 2002, was often called the luckiest guy in football. He always seemed to be in the right place at the right time for the interception or tackle. What Darrell liked to point out is that you make your own luck. What he was describing is the odds-tilting effects of hard work, preparation, a positive attitude, and incredible speed (clocked at 10.08 seconds in the 100-meter dash in 1982; for comparison purposes, the 1980 Olympic gold medal 100-meter dash time was 10.25 seconds).

In investment terms, Darrell's NFL Hall of Fame streak-creating behavior could be described as preparation and discipline. Reading this book is your preparation. Staying on plan is the necessary discipline.

There is no question that you can improve your odds of having a winning streak even when it comes to winning the lottery. Your odds of winning the lottery increase if you buy a ticket versus the odds for people who do not buy a ticket:

1. It is important to place yourself in the right place. Think of a soccer game. If you are not a player on the field, you will have a hard time scoring a goal legally. Once you are on the field, if you are near the opponent's goal and away from defenders when the ball is kicked to you, your chances of scoring go up even more. Your position in life has an impact on randomness. Darrell Green of the Washington Redskins was a master of creating his own luck.

2. Once you are in position, you should be ready to recognize and act on a positive or negative streak. You should have thought about this possible outcome in advance and developed a plan to take advantage of the streak.

The nature of randomness gives us a mathematical expectation that streaks will occur. The reason bias is important is that it can make streaks persist in a predictable way. To say this world is either absolutely random or deterministic is unnecessary to getting rich in the stock market. It is clearly a combination of the two.

CHAPTER THREE

Why Should We Invest?

W E SHOULD invest for the following reasons:

1. We are likely to live a long time.
2. We are unlikely to be employed for our entire lives.
3. Our income and expenses are unlikely to always match up perfectly.
4. Social Security, pension plans, and other retirement funds are becoming a less reliable source of funds for retirement.
5. Investing can allow us to capture the powerful wealth-building effects of compounding.

Modern people (the set of all people alive today) have certain traits that require modern finance. According to the U.S. Department of Health and Human Resources, Americans who were born in 1900 had a life expectancy at birth of 49.2 years. This made the requirement to save for retirement somewhat unnecessary on average because in so many cases there was no retirement.

Today, Americans can expect to live into their eighties. This is creating a strain on a safety net system built on out-of-date assumptions. It has raised the cost of healthcare enormously. It is straining pension plans and the Social Security system. When the original Social Security Act was passed in 1935, the life expectancy at birth of the average American was roughly 62 years. Social Security benefits were meant to cover just a few years of life. No one considered the consequences of people living 20 years longer on average and what that would do to both the benefit burden and the ratio of young to old by which the number of old needing support would overwhelm the relatively smaller number of young providing the support.

Fidelity Investments estimates that a 65-year-old couple retiring in 2012 should plan on spending $240,000 out of pocket on healthcare, assuming the man lives 17 more years and the woman lives 20. Year over year, this estimated expense has increased 6 percent. Medicare pays for an average of just 51 percent of healthcare costs according to the Employee Benefit Research Institute.

Jobs for life have become a thing of the past. The labor markets are far more dynamic today than ever before. If they can make it cheaper in India or China, there goes your job. If a guy out of school knows the new technology better than you do, there goes your job even if you have valuable business experience. If a new technology comes along that makes your company and industry obsolete, there goes your job. Not only do you have to run faster and faster on the employment treadmill, you have to jump from one treadmill to another with increasing frequency.

If you work for a state or municipal government entity that has promised an attractive lifelong retirement package, do not let your guard down. States and cities are under tremendous financial pressure. With taxpayers less willing to pay higher taxes, particularly when unemployment is high and disposable income is not increasing, governments have started the politically ugly process of pulling back on those promised benefits. Some pension adjustments are already occurring. Recent elections in San Jose and San Diego, California, mandate reductions in the pensions of government employees. Wisconsin's failed gubernatorial recall of Scott Walker, who stripped collective bargaining rights from many public employees, provides a clear indication that voters may not keep paying expected pension obligations. Voided private pensions of auto and auto parts suppliers after the Lehman Brothers collapse in 2008 may be a forerunner of things to come in the public sector. At the end of the day, all of us need to plan to take care of ourselves no matter what we paid into the system or what was promised. A survey conducted by the Employee Benefit Research Institute indicates that in 1991, 11 percent of workers said they expected to retire after age 65. In 2012, that percentage increased to 37 percent.

Modern finance theory is all about creating an investment strategy that will maximize your ability to not outlive your savings. Achieving the objective of having your savings support you comfortably for your entire life is the purpose of this book.

CHAPTER FOUR

The Story of Mr. M

W E KNOW another guy. This guy is one of the most colorful people we know. He loves to tell his story. We have heard his stories for years. His life story is incredible. We feel lucky to know him, be his friend, and share a part of his story.

He likes to say he has lived in the best of times. Looking back, it sure was. It was 1950 when his career was starting, and the biggest gold rush California had ever experienced was just getting under way. The value created from the real estate boom in California makes the gold rush of 1849 look like a flake instead of a nugget. There were roughly 10 million people living in the state in 1950. Over the next 50 years, that number would quadruple. The average price of a home in California in 1950 was $9,564. By 2000, it was $211,000, up 2,106 percent.

What is different about Mr. M is that he immediately recognized the strong secular real-estate price trend and took full advantage of it. When he started in 1950, he had $500. Financially, he was not well positioned to make a fortune in real estate. Mentally, he was in a perfect place because he had an open mind and an eagerness to fully pursue the opportunity.

Mr. M could not have felt better. He felt blessed for having met his wife and lucky to be alive. In World War II, he had enlisted in the Navy and was trained as a landing craft captain. His company was assigned to participate in the first American offensive in the central Pacific region. The objective was to island-hop across the Pacific, establishing forward air bases that would eventually support a full-on invasion of Japan.

Before leaving the country, the company was formed into two lines on the basis of the sailors' last names for immunization shots. Those with names beginning A through L received their medication and were ready for action. Those with names beginning M through Z received a bad batch of immunization shots, making that half of the company deathly ill.

Many died of fever in the hospital. Mr. M's doctors had given up on him. In what felt like a final request, he asked for a large glass of pineapple juice. He spent his last night in the hospital downing the juice. In the morning, he walked out thinner but at a normal body temperature.

The members of the first group were assigned to operate landing craft in the Battle of Tarawa, which took place in November 1943. There were 4,500 well-prepared and -supplied Japanese ready to repel the landing. Tarawa was the most fortified atoll the United States would invade during the Pacific Campaign. They fought to almost the last man. In a space of 76 hours, nearly 6,000 Japanese and Americans died on that tiny island.

The Navy ordered the attack 30 minutes early. As the landing craft headed for the beach, they discovered that the tide had not risen enough to allow their boats to clear the coral reef. The supporting naval bombardment had been lifted to allow the Marines to land. With the landing craft stuck on the reef and the big American guns silent, the Japanese concentrated their forces and intensified their fire on those boats. Killing landing craft operators was a great way to disable an entire boatload of Marines. Mr. M's company of landing craft captains with names ending in A through L for the most part never made it home. The Marines gave up on the boats and waded for hundreds of yards through chest-high water and intense enemy fire to the beach.

Mr. M, whose last name ends with a vowel, had another reason to feel blessed. His father, who had a sixth-grade education but a PhD in life, had found the future Mrs. M through relatives in Italy. In the late 1940s, Mr. M's family moved from Los Angeles to San Francisco. Mr. M remained behind in Los Angeles to complete college after the war. In 1949, Mr. M's father instructed Mr. M to sell the house in LA, move to San Francisco, and meet this special lady. In 1950, Mr. and Mrs. M were married and now have been happily married for over 60 years. For Mr. M, 1950 was a great year, and he was ready to take on the world.

In San Francisco, Mr. M secured a job with a small real estate company. His first assignment was to sell 10 acres in Newark, California. In 1950 Newark was almost entirely empty farmland. Even the most optimistic forecasts did not show development of the area for decades. Mr. M found a buyer. What struck Mr. M as odd was that the buyer was in his middle seventies and unlikely to benefit from any near-term price appreciation. When Mr. M asked him why he was buying the land, he advised Mr. M that "you don't get rich selling property, you get rich buying property."

This conversation changed Mr. M's life. He realized he had to be an owner rather than a property broker. Having sold his parents' home in Los Angeles, he knew that the trajectory of California real estate pricing was up.

Back in San Francisco, Mr. M went to work right away on figuring out how he could become a property owner. He asked around about who he should talk with regarding buying real estate. He was told to talk with a barber on Union Street who dabbled in real estate speculation on the side. The barber told him about a deal on the corner of Union and Laguna that included two flats and a bar and said that Mr. M could go in as an equal partner. Mr. M scraped together his $3,500 half of the financial commitment from his father and friends. Sight unseen and on the instructions of the barber, Mr. M bought the property.

In less than a year, the barber and Mr. M were able to sell the two flats for their original investment. Mr. M paid back his lenders. Shortly thereafter, they sold the bar for nearly $45,000. He now had over $22,500 in his pocket, up from $500.

Shortly after completing the deal with the barber, Mr. M drove down Howard Street. Mr. M almost never drove down Howard Street. As he passed the Del Monte Meat Company, an acquaintance jumped into the street, waving Mr. M down. He had a deal. If Mr. M could pay him $15,000 before the end of the business day—about an hour—he could take ownership of the hotel next to the meat company. Mr. M said yes, again sight unseen.

The next day, Mr. M discovered that he had purchased a 60-room hotel with three bathrooms, one for each floor. Not having the capital to develop the property, he turned around and sold it for slightly more than what he had paid with a kicker: the buyer threw in 10 acres in Hemet, California.

Mr. M had never heard of Hemet. Hemet is a tiny town out in the southern California desert near San Jacinto and Palm Springs. In 1950, Mr. M was simply connecting the dots in his life. Already, $500 had grown to roughly $22,500. To connect the next dot, Mr. M drove south to Hemet to take a look.

The Alessandro Hotel was on the southwest corner of Florida Avenue and Harvard Street in Hemet. On the ground floor was a small real estate office.

After a good night's rest, Mr. M walked through the lobby and into the real estate office to see if the guys in the office knew anything about his property. When he showed them the location, they immediately offered him $40,000 for the property. Mr. M couldn't believe it. They raised their offer to $50,000. Mr. M sold it on the spot.

The original $500 was now $72,500. The streak was on. Mr. M knew a good run when he saw it, and it was time to step it up. Three property trades turned into 500 more property trades. Rather than working with barbers and guys standing next to the meat factory, he moved in with wealthy entrepreneurs. His small apartment on 9th Avenue in a fourplex became a 20,000-square-foot mansion in one of the most exclusive neighborhoods in the San Francisco Bay Area. By age 35, Mr. M was set for life.

Although millions of Californians were exposed to the multidecade real estate boom and were fully aware of it, most participated only through ownership of a primary residence. Some owned second homes or one or two income properties. A few made a fortune. Mr. M saw and understood the trend and went all in. In 1950, many Americans' views on investing were heavily dominated by memories of the Great Depression. The 1930s and 1940s had not been easy times. Mr. M, in contrast, felt he had nothing to lose. His mind was open to investing aggressively in areas where the risk/reward balance was favorable.

Not only was Mr. M aware of a strong, secular market trend, he understood how the inner workings of the market could offer him an advantage. The real estate market in the 1950s was far from efficient. Real estate transactions in San Francisco were published and distributed in a small booklet every morning from city hall. The best way to know what was going on in the market was to read the booklet daily. Only a small number of people bothered to do this. Mr. M had a tremendous information advantage. Sellers often mispriced buildings as they did not thoroughly know market pricing and rental trends.

Mr. M Takeaways

The first important takeaway from the Mr. M story is that when a hot streak comes, it is important to "do enough to make a difference." Mr. M was mentally ready to commit all he had to the real estate boom. After a few initial transactions, he had the capital to go all in. The barber, in contrast, continued to dabble and ended his career as a barber on Union Street. When a streak presents itself, many people find it difficult to leave their comfort zone and take full advantage of the opportunity that presents itself. The barber stayed attached to his chair.

It is also important to recognize how markets operate. Mr. M could identify opportunities because he had a better understanding of the market than did many of the people selling to him because he read the daily transaction booklet. In addition to understanding the short-term market dynamics better, Mr. M was comfortable with the secular trend. Mr. M knew that in a bullish market, it was unlikely that he was at risk of losing a lot of money. This enabled him to move quickly and take advantage of opportunities as they presented themselves.

In the stock market, it is important to understand the longer-term trends. During the 1980s and 1990s, investors could buy almost any stock without any due diligence and make money over time. The market was enjoying its largest bull run of the century. Over the last

12 years, the chances of not making money from stock ownership have been high. When the market is in a sideways, choppy trend, it is essential for investors to recognize the nature of the investment landscape and take an investment approach that will work in the current market conditions.

CHAPTER FIVE

Building Blocks

FOR MOST individual investors, investable securities are usually defined as fixed income (bonds) or equities (stocks). Much of the time, retail investors who buy bonds are interested in collecting interest payments rather than speculating on changes in the underlying bond value. With stocks, investors generally are looking for capital appreciation rather than income.

In thinking about investible securities, few investors think about holding cash as putting money to work. However, there are times when the relative strength of cash is far greater than that of stocks and bonds. In major down markets, cash is king. We like to include cash, along with stocks and bonds, as an asset class investors should consider in their overall portfolio allocation.

a. Money "M"

U.S. dollars (USD) are born at the U.S. Department of the Treasury. We print them (mint them if we are talking about coins). This is a basic answer to the question, "Mommy, where does money come from?" The printed/minted money you carry in your wallet is called M0. If you put your money in a checking account, it is now called M1. As money is placed into decreasingly accessible places such as savings accounts, it is progressively classified as M2, M3, and MZM. There is also MB, which is all the paper currency, including coins and bills in bank vaults and Federal Reserve (Fed) Bank credit. In order of liquidity, the list goes M0, MB, M1, M2, M3, and MZM.

M2 is the measure of money that most economists track. It includes U.S. Department of the Treasury printed money and the money supply created by the Federal Reserve as it lends to banks by buying bonds.

The Fed can play with the money supply in a wide variety of ways. To avoid getting bogged down in the minutiae of Fed policy options, the Fed controls the money supply essentially by changing short-term borrowing rates and by buying and selling debt. The Fed's manipulation of the money supply is called monetary policy.

An increase in the supply of money typically lowers interest rates, which in turn usually generates more investment and places more money in the hands of consumers, stimulating consumption. Businesses respond by ordering more raw materials and increasing production. The increased business activity raises the demand for labor. Wages rise, and a positive bullish economic cycle is under way.

Economic growth may contract if the money supply is constricted. Currently, the Federal Reserve through its monetary policy is attempting to achieve roughly a 2 percent inflation rate and an unemployment rate below 6.5 percent. With the Fed wanting more robust economic growth, it is increasing the money supply. If inflation exceeds certain threshold levels, the Fed may restrict the money supply.

The Federal Reserve is becoming increasingly public about what financial targets it is attempting to achieve through monetary policy. We are writing this book in the wake of the 2008–2009 credit crisis when economic recovery is slow, the labor market is slack, and global economic conditions raise threats of recession and deflation. As conditions change, it is likely that the Fed will modify its stated economic objectives over time.

It may sound like the Federal Reserve has tight control over the money supply. It does not. What is outside the Fed's ability to control directly is the velocity of money, which has a powerful influence on the effective money supply.

The velocity of money is a measure of people's willingness to spend it. If we are confident that our incomes are stable or growing, we are usually willing to spend money. As we all spend money, the velocity of money flowing through our economic system increases, and this is effectively an increase in the money supply. This is all good for economic activity. If we are worried about our incomes, particularly relative to our fixed expenses, we tend to hold on to our money. Declining money velocity is equivalent to a decrease in the money supply. This is not good for economic growth.

Figure 5.1 is a chart of the velocity of money (money multiplier) from 2003 through March 2013. You can see that every dollar in the economy turned over roughly 8.5× from 2003 until the heart of the credit crisis in the second half of 2008. This pace of spending had been roughly constant. Rather than returning to "normalized" levels years after the crisis, the money multiplier has shrunk even further from roughly 4.6× to 3.6×.

The velocity of money is partly why we focus on understanding consumer and investor sentiment. If sentiment is improving (risk perceptions are falling), it is likely that money velocity and economic activity will also improve. If sentiment is declining (perceptions of risk are rising), this is likely to have a negative impact on the economy and equity markets.

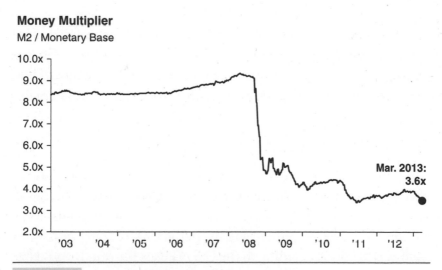

Money Multiplier
M2 / Monetary Base

FIGURE 5.1 Money Multiplier 2003–March 2013

Source: J.P. Morgan Asset Management.

Although the U.S. federal government and the Federal Reserve can try to "talk markets up" by making encouraging remarks about the economy or making clear to investors their policy objectives, investor sentiment is out of their direct control. With sentiment playing a material role in money velocity, the levers the government has at its disposal to control the money supply are not complete. When they spin their dials, the linkage is loose.

Money Supply Takeaways. Generally, a rising money supply is bullish for stocks and a decreasing money supply is bearish for stocks. As an investor, always try to have the wind at your back. If you are long equities, you will benefit from an expansion in U.S. and global liquidity conditions. In the aftermath of the 2008–2009 credit crisis, much of the U.S. stock market advance has been attributed to a loosening of credit conditions by the Federal Reserve through its bond buying programs called quantitative easing.

Market sentiment has an impact on money supply through the velocity of money. As a stock investor, paying attention to market sentiment can help you determine whether the market is likely to be bullish or bearish in the near term to intermediate term.

Like almost everything involving government action and economic policy, the linkage between the action and the reaction is not direct. This adds to the complexity of forecasting the market. Change in the money supply is an important variable in the equation of how stocks will behave going forward, but it is not the only variable.

b. The Cost of Money: Interest

The primary risk of owning money is loss of real buying power in the future as a result of inflation. Paper currencies can be devalued by oversupply and/or broad economic inflationary trends. As an example, the average price of a home in the United States in January 1970 was $23,600 according to the U.S. Census Bureau. If you'd had $23,600 in cash in 1970 and decided to place your cash in the mattress and wait until today to buy a home, you would be shocked to discover that the average price of a home is now well above $230,000, 10 times what you would have paid in 1970. This is called inflation.

If you had purchased an asset that collected interest of roughly 5.6 percent and compounded the gains rather than sticking the money in the mattress, your 1970 money would have kept pace with house price inflation and you would have roughly $230,000 of buying power today to buy the house.

The way investors are compensated for the time value of their money is that they receive interest.

Interest is the price of a dollar. In addition to collecting interest on money to keep pace with inflation, investors usually require an extra return if they take on extra risk. All financial investments are measured by their return relative to their risk. The benchmark for measuring investments is the interest rate paid on U.S. Treasuries. Because the United States can simply print the money, U.S. Treasury rates provide an indication of the pure cost of money because the risk of not getting paid back is assumed to be essentially zero.

By knowing the riskless cost of money (the interest rate on short-term Treasuries), you can determine what amount of excess return you are receiving to compensate you for additional risk you may be taking in any particular investment. If you are not making at least the riskless rate of return, you may want to consider not making the investment.

The Cost of Money Takeaways. Interest rates are an essential element of the investment landscape. The riskless rate of return is used to benchmark almost all financial investments.

Interest rate trends are important. If interest rates are rising, you will want higher returns from your investments. If interest rates are falling, you might be willing to accept lower returns. In the wake of the 2008–2009 credit crisis, the 10-year Treasury rate fell below 1.4 percent, its lowest level on record. With interest rates that low, the threshold for finding other investments attractive was set at a very low level. This helps explain how low interest rates can stimulate investment in stocks and a wide variety of other risky assets.

Who wants a 1.4 percent return over 10 years? Investors will attempt to do better by taking on some risk. Declining interest rates from 1982 (the 10-year Treasury rate on January 1, 1982, was roughly 14.5 percent) through 2012 help explain the 30-year bull market in bonds.

Understanding what is going on with interest rates is an important element of understanding the stock market. For the moment, we have briefly mentioned that interest rates vary in relationship to risk—more risk, more interest—and how interest rate trends can affect stock and bond prices. The major missing piece with regard to interest rates and the way they relate to stock market movement is the amount of spread between various interest rates. Interest rate spreads are useful for determining collective investor risk appetite. We discuss this in Chapter 14.

c. Gold

With many developed countries currently swamped in debt, there is an incentive to create inflation. If a future dollar becomes cheap relative to the value of a dollar today, governments can effectively lower the real cost of debt. The face amount on a loan is not adjusted higher to account for the effects of inflation, and loans by definition are paid back some time in the future.

Part of the explanation of why gold has appreciated strongly over the last decade is that gold is viewed by many as a world currency that cannot be devalued by government printing presses. Put another way, the supply of gold is relatively stable whereas the supply of paper currencies can fluctuate dramatically depending on the unpredictable behavior of governments.

As the Federal Reserve has continued to expand the money supply through its quantitative easing programs, gold and related investments have performed well. In 2011, Utah became the first U.S. state since the Depression to make gold and silver coins legal tender again. Metal coins can be exchanged for their market value. More than a dozen other states, including Minnesota, Idaho, Georgia, and Missouri, have considered similar laws.

The difficulty of valuing gold is due to the fact that more than half of total gold demand comes from the jewelry market. Roughly 67 percent of total demand for gold is driven by the jewelry and technology markets. Both markets are price-sensitive and are able to use gold substitutes. In other words, the supply-constrained world currency aspect of the gold valuation is less than half the story. This makes trends in gold prices somewhat unpredictable.

Figure 5.2 is a long-term chart of gold prices. Gold reached a peak price in January 1980. It is the only major investment asset category we are aware of that is still below its peak price from more than 30 years ago. From 1980 to 1985, gold prices declined by 67 percent.

Gold Takeaways. If you have a bearish perspective and/or you believe that the value of paper currencies will erode over time, you might want to consider having some gold in your portfolio. It is clear that gold performs well in situations in which a currency undergoes dramatic deflation. For example, in 1998 the Russian government devalued the ruble, defaulted on domestic debt, and declared a moratorium on payment to foreign creditors. Inflation reached 84 percent that year. Those who owned rubles were wiped out, but those who owned gold sidestepped a disaster.

Apart from disaster scenarios, there is disagreement about the importance of including gold in one's portfolio. It is clear from the price action from 1980 to 1985 and during the spring of 2013, when gold declined by approximately 30 percent, that the gold market is subject to dramatic price swings. All financial securities can experience overcrowded trades and speculative investing.

d. Bonds

We live in a debt world. As consumers, we borrow to buy cars, TVs, houses, and so forth. We almost all use credit cards. As businesses, we use short-term borrowing to make payrolls and buy inventory from which to make finished goods. Both businesses and consumers often carry lines of credit. Municipalities and states issue bonds to finance a

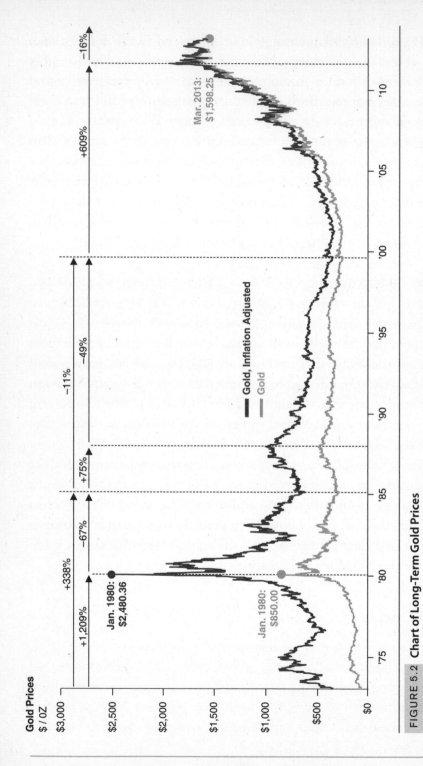

Gold Prices
$ / OZ

FIGURE 5.2 Chart of Long-Term Gold Prices

Source: Eco Win, BLS, U.S. Department of Energy, Fact Set, J.P. Morgan Asset Management CPI adjusted gold values are calculated using monthly averages of gold spot prices divided by the CPI value for that month. CPI is rebased to 100 at the end of the chart Returns based on nominal prices. Data are as of 3/31/13.

wide variety of both infrastructure (schools, roads, sewer systems, etc.) and regular-way business needs. As we know, the federal government spends more than it makes in tax revenue and is highly dependent on the Treasury Department's regular debt auctions for funding. Our economy relies on free-flowing debt markets. Debt is the WD-40 of capitalism.

The total size of the U.S. debt market is roughly $32 trillion, not counting derivatives. When one adds derivatives, the debt market is orders of magnitude larger. At the peak in 2008, the nominal value of all credit default swap contracts (a derivate of debt) was roughly $55 trillion. The total size of the U.S. equity market is roughly $15 trillion. When the debt market has a problem (e.g., the 2008–2009 credit crisis), it is likely that the equity market will have a problem as well.

In contrast, when credit is easy to obtain (rates are low, M2 is expanding, velocity is healthy, and banks are highly willing and able to lend), you should expect strong equity markets. Money borrowed by consumers and companies finds its way into equities through increased economic activity (remodeling the house, new appliances, etc.) and via corporate stock buybacks, capital investment, mergers and acquisitions, and dividends.

As an investor, you can buy a wide variety of bonds, including government and corporate bonds. The interest you receive should compensate you for the risk that the loan will not be paid back in full (default risk) and for your opportunity cost. Your opportunity cost is the money you are not making in other possible investments as a result of having made this loan.

In the big picture, one of the safest loans you can make is to the U.S. government. Lending to the government involves buying U.S. Treasury bills (less than 1 year term), notes (1- to 10-year terms), or bonds (more than 10 years to maturity). U.S. Treasury bills, notes, and bonds are called Treasuries, and they represent the ultimate "risk-off" trade. The reason U.S. Treasuries are considered relatively free from default risk is that the U.S. Treasury can simply print more dollars to pay back its debt.

When major institutional investors around the world are afraid, they tend to buy U.S. Treasuries. When there is a stampede of Treasury buyers, the U.S. government does not need to offer a relatively high rate of return (interest rate/yield) to sell its debt. This explains why U.S. Treasury yields were hitting all-time low levels during the European sovereign debt crisis. Investors around the world were scared of virtually everything else (including the possible collapse of the euro) more than they were scared of receiving little to negative real returns (nominal yield minus inflation equals real yield) with U.S. Treasuries.

Lending to government entities can have a broad risk profile. Beyond Treasuries, there is an active debt market for municipal and state debt. Depending on what is offered as collateral for these bonds, yields vary. General obligation bonds that require that the bonds be paid with tax revenues are usually considered less risky than specific project bonds that are dependent on the success of a particular project as the source of backing.

Corporate debt can reside farther out on the risk spectrum. Corporate debt ranges from investment grade (low risk) to junk (high risk). As the perceived risk level of the debt rises, so do the debt yields. Because corporate debt is more risky than Treasuries, it generally has higher yields.

Bond returns are usually less volatile than stock returns. This is the case because bondholders give away potential upside by agreeing to a rate of return up front and because bonds reside higher up in the capital structure than stocks. As a result, the long-term average volatility (standard deviation) of investment-grade corporate bonds is about 4 percent (calculated by Rydex/SGI using data from Bloomberg) compared with roughly 21 percent for stocks.

It is important to know who gets what when a company fails because it affects the nature of how a security will trade. This is what we mean when we talk about bonds residing higher up in the capital structure than stocks. If you are a secured bondholder of a company and the company files for bankruptcy, you will have a claim on the assets that were used to back the loan. This is exactly the same idea as a bank lending you money to buy a house that is secured by the house. If you fail to pay the bank its money, it can take your house and sell it to recover the principal and interest. Technically, a default event is usually triggered when an interest payment is missed.

If you are an unsecured bondholder—you lent money without tying the loan to some specific asset or security—you will have to wait to see what is left after the secured lenders collect before you can determine what you might recover. Because you do not have a specific claim on an asset, you have taken on more risk. The good news is that your claim as an unsecured bondholder comes before claims made by equity owners. Also, you should have received higher interest payments than the secured lenders did when the loan was performing for taking on the added risk of making an unsecured loan.

As a stockholder in a failed company, you are the last in line in terms of collecting what is left of the company's net assets. Shareholders own both the assets and the liabilities of a company whereas bondholders are exposed only to the company's assets. Much of the time in a default situation, there is nothing left for the stockholders to recover after the bondholders have been paid. Because stocks are lower down in the capital structure than bonds, stockholders take on more risk than do bondholders. As stocks theoretically have unlimited upside and the possibility of trading down to zero, they tend to be more volatile than bonds, which have a predetermined payout and a lower probability of trading to zero.

It is reasonable to take on more risk in an investment if you are likely to receive more reward. Excess return from stocks over bonds is called the equity risk premium. Over the long run, stock investors expect to receive a higher return than bondholders because of the equity risk premium.

The bond market tends to be characterized as a momentum market. Buying propels more buying, and selling propels more selling. The momentum nature of the bond market makes bond market blowups spectacular. The most recent spectacular bond market blowup was the credit crisis that began in the U.S. subprime mortgage market in 2007. At the height of the crisis, many U.S. corporations faced imminent bankruptcy as they were unable to obtain short-term financing for their working capital needs.

The credit cycle is a very important piece of understanding the equity cycle. Credit cycles typically last for several years. Since 2009, the credit markets have been booming (companies are raising record amounts of capital by selling debt at historically low rates), which is good for stocks. During the 2009–2012 bond boom, the S&P 500 more than doubled from its March 2009 low. Debt capital raised by corporations often finds its way into the equity market via stock buybacks, mergers and acquisitions, or dividends.

Bond Takeaways. From the standpoint of an equity investor, knowing what is going on in the bond markets is important. Capital raised by corporations from borrowing activities often finds its way into the equity market. Companies can grow faster and offer a higher return on capital when the debt market is free flowing and interest rates are low. Tightening credit conditions have the opposite effect.

Government borrowing can help stimulate economic activity in the short term but can crowd out private sector investment and government discretionary spending over longer periods. High debt levels maintained by the federal government raise concerns about the long-term expected growth rates for the U.S. economy as tax levels may be elevated and spending other than on debt service by the government may be reduced. Additionally, high debt levels can potentially lead to rising interest rates as bond buyers demand a higher return in light of escalating risk.

Bond derivative markets make understanding what is going on in the bond market somewhat tricky. Warren Buffett called them "financial weapons of mass destruction." Credit default swap (CDS) contracts, essentially insurance that the debt and interest will be paid back, can greatly magnify the impact of a default. When Lehman Brothers failed, the cost of honoring its CDS obligations helped drive AIG into bankruptcy. AIG required a nearly $200 billion government bailout. Major financial institutions (Bank of America, JPMorgan Chase, Goldman Sachs, etc.) had poor visibility into the debt derivative world and struggled to accurately measure counterparty risk as CDSs were private party contracts.

Counterparty risk is a way of saying banks were not sure if they or their business partners would still be in business the next morning. With the financial sector suffering a pressing "going concern" risk, the securities markets collapsed and the S&P 500 fell from high to low by more than 50 percent.

Although there have been some improvements in financial visibility and controls in the bond derivatives markets, the situation is far from perfect. Risk stemming from this area can be a powerful source of negative pressure on equity prices.

Properly functioning credit markets are essential for the stock market to behave rationally. During the 2008–2009 credit crisis, bondholders became concerned that their advantaged position in the capital structure was not going to be honored by the U.S. government in some of its bailout activities. A loss of faith in the legal protections granted to bondholders during this time was potentially catastrophic for securities trading generally. Part of the reason the bond and equity markets recovered in the wake of the credit crisis was that the capital structure of our economic system was generally upheld during the time of crisis.

e. Stocks

When you own a stock, you own a share of a company. Because you are a company owner through your stock holdings, modern financial theory says you should care about earnings and dividends. Unlike a bondholder, you have full exposure to potential upside and downside associated with the company performing better or worse than expected. Generally, the theory goes, as earnings and dividends rise, the value of your stock ownership should appreciate. Earnings have a positive correlation with stock prices. Partly because expected earnings and dividends can be volatile, stock returns are usually more volatile than bond returns. The average annual volatility (standard deviation) of stocks over the long run is about 21 percent.

As with bonds, there are a wide variety of stocks. Stocks are most often categorized as value or growth and by size measured by market capitalization. Market capitalization is calculated by multiplying shares outstanding by the current share price. Sizes are most often described as small, mid, and large cap. Although there is no set industry standard, small-cap stocks generally have market caps ranging from about $300 million to $2 billion, mid-cap stocks are $2 to $10 billion, and large-cap stocks are often defined as greater than $10 billion. Small cap growth stocks are considered aggressive, in contrast to large cap value stocks, which are often viewed as defensive. Investor sentiment can be measured to some extent by which types of stocks are showing relative strength.

Stocks use the same basic elements of expected payouts and time to establish price as do bonds. What complicates the pricing of stocks is that company earnings and dividends have much higher variability than do bond payouts in normal circumstances. Stock prices reflect a full array of future possible earnings outcomes multiplied by the probability that each specific outcome may occur. The probability-weighted payouts outcome is then discounted back to today's prices. This discounting is most often done by applying a price/earnings (P/E) multiple to company earnings.

Figure 5.3 shows adjusted after-tax corporate profits as a percentage of gross domestic product (GDP) from 1960 to June 30, 2011. Figure 5.4 is a graph of the S&P 500 index from 1997 through March 31, 2013.

What the two charts make clear when viewed side by side is that there is a positive correlation between earnings and stock values but that the linkage between the two is not perfectly one to one. In terms of positive correlation, earnings and stocks peaked in 2000 and 2007, which is a nice match. Both stocks and earnings were rising from lows in 1993. Earnings collapsed in 2002 and 2008, which matches the valleys in the stock chart.

However, S&P 500 earnings have roughly doubled both on an absolute basis and as a percentage of GDP since 2000. At the end of 2012 the S&P 500 was trading at about where it had been in 2000 even though earnings had doubled. It is evident that something other than earnings is responsible for a great deal of stock movement.

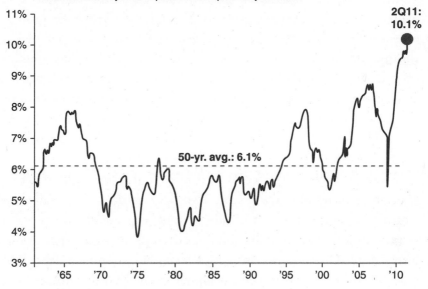

Adjusted After-Tax Corporate Profits (% of GDP)

Includes inventory and capital consumption adjustments

FIGURE 5.3 Adjusted After-Tax Corporate Profits, 1960–June 2011

Source: U.S. Bureau of Economic Analysis, Factset.

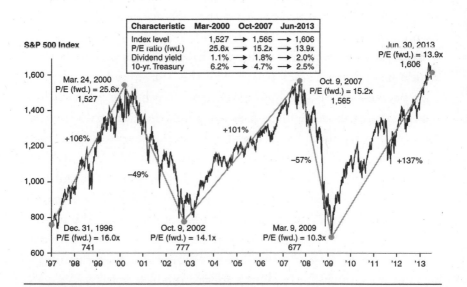

FIGURE 5.4 The S&P 500, 1997–March 2013

Source: Standard & Poor's, First Call, Compustat, FactSet, J.P. Morgan Asset Management.

Investor sentiment and perceptions of risk play a role in the way stocks are valued in addition to earnings. The sentiment shifts are expressed in P/E terms as follows: In 2000, forward earnings growth rates were perceived to be accelerating as the world was experiencing the digital and Internet revolutions. Money was flooding into equities both in the public markets and through private equity venture firms as an 18-year bull market harmonically mated with a tremendous surge in technology advancement. Investor eagerness to own stocks was high. The S&P 500 P/E was near 28X on S&P 500 earnings of $56.13. The S&P 500 peaked on March 24, 2000, at about 1,553.

Twelve years later, the S&P 500 P/E had fallen to roughly a P/E of 14X on earnings of roughly $105. Two bear markets and a financial world seemingly out of control caused many eager equity investors to suffer for more than a decade. Forward earnings growth expectations were subdued by concerns about high levels of government debt globally. The rise of terrorism and instability in the Middle East elevated perceptions of geopolitical risk. The lack of stock price appreciation and increased volatility did much to squelch the appetite for stocks. Individual investors pulled money on a net basis from U.S. equity mutual funds for five straight years through 2011, the longest streak on record.

Yale economics professor Robert Shiller wrote a paper in 1981 in which he compared stock prices with the discounted cash flows of a corporation (measured by the dividends). What he determined is that stock prices move up and down much more than do the cash flows that are supposed to be driving them. Because stock prices way overshoot or undershoot discounted cash flows, Shiller concluded that market pricing is not efficient. Whether we want to describe the market as efficient after noticing that stock movement is often not proportional with earnings movement is not the point. The point is that Shiller was on to something when he stated that there might be other factors that are potentially more important than earnings in driving stock prices in the short and intermediate terms.

When you invert the price/earnings ratio, you get the earnings/price ratio, or the earnings yield of stocks. When investors are anxious about the risks associated with owning stocks, they demand a higher expected rate of return (earnings yield) to buy stocks. The P/E is depressed. When investors are complacent about risk, they require a lower expected return to own stocks and be exposed to the risks of stock ownership. The P/E appreciates. P/E ratios and the prices of stocks are materially affected by investor sentiment. In fact, during the 12 years beginning in 2000, investor sentiment had a far larger influence on stock price than did earnings.

Figure 5.5 is a chart of the S&P 500 earnings yield and Baa bond yield from 1994 through March 2013. As of March 2013, stock risk was perceived as high relative to medium-grade bond risk as measured by relative yield of the two security types. Over time, it is evident that the perceived risk of owning bonds and stocks is not a constant and is subject to significant volatility.

True to theory, equities as an asset class have generally had a higher return than have lower-risk bonds over long periods. Since 1912, stocks have had an average annual real return (nominal return minus inflation equals real return) of about 7 percent. What we show later in this book is that using long-term average returns as your investment guide can be very misleading and disappointing.

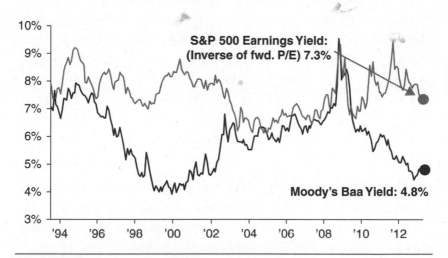

FIGURE 5.5 S&P Earnings Yield vs. Baa Bond Yield

Source: J.P. Morgan Asset Management.

Stock Takeaways. Ultimately, this book is about following a discipline to make money through stock investing with a safety-first approach. So far, we have learned that stocks carry risk, can be volatile, and are influenced by a variety of factors. In later chapters we will add an in-depth array of real-world market factors and academic theory to further define the trading pressures stocks are subjected to that will affect the ways you can make money in the market.

In a world where investors are flooded every day with mostly negative news by an increasingly omnipresent media industry, it can be difficult to see through the clutter and form a balanced opinion about the stock market. One of the best indicators of the health of the market is the market itself. If the market is in a bullish, upward trend, it is likely that this trend will continue for some time. If the market is in a bearish, downward trend, it is likely that this trend will continue for some time. The market tends to streak.

f. Confidence in Stocks

At the end of 2012, three years after the credit crisis stock market bottom, investor confidence in the stock market was near all-time lows. In the Chicago Booth/Kellogg School quarterly survey for the second quarter of 2012, 79 percent of the survey respondents did not trust the U.S. financial system, which is about where the lack of trust was in March 2009. Many people have become increasingly convinced that the stock market is not a reflection of pricing efficiency but more a reflection of pricing manipulation, greed, and a corrupt system that strongly favors institutional insiders.

Over the last decade or so, investors have been subjected to the following:

- The stock market crash of March 2000 to October 2002 (dot-com bubble) leading to a loss of $5 trillion of market capitalization. The Nasdaq Composite (with a high percentage of technology stocks) plunged by roughly 80 percent from high to low.
- The September 11, 2001, terrorist attack, which has forever changed how we live our lives in the United States and closed

the NYSE for four trading days. (Keeping stock markets closed for four consecutive days, even including a weekend, is an unusual event in the United States.)

- The fraud and collapse of Enron. This was a multi-billion-dollar company built on opaque, speculative off-balance-sheet financing. The company went from being the seventh largest revenue company in the Fortune 500 to zero in about one year. The collapse of Enron also meant the collapse of Arthur Andersen, the fifth largest accounting firm in the world at that time.

- In addition to Enron, there were significant corporate accounting scandals at Tyco International, Adelphia, Peregrine Systems, and WorldCom. These cases of fraud contributed to the passage of the Sarbanes-Oxley Act of 2002 (aka the Public Company Accounting Reform and Investor Protection Act and the Corporate and Auditing Accountability and Responsibility Act).

- The 2008–2009 credit crisis when the S&P 500 dropped by more than 50 percent from high to low. A system built on easy credit, derivatives, and lack of financial controls led to the Great Recession and nearly caused a depression. Many supposedly safe stocks such as Fannie Mae, Freddie Mac, General Electric, and AIG and many of the major banks nearly or completely collapsed.

- The Bernie Madoff Ponzi scheme involving the defrauding of thousands of investors of billions of dollars (roughly $50 billion). Madoff was a former chairman of the Nasdaq stock market. The Madoff incident was closely followed by Allen Stanford of Stanford Financial Group and Jon Corzine of MF Global, who also defrauded thousands of investors of billions of dollars. Corzine was a former CEO of Goldman Sachs and governor of New Jersey.

- The May 6, 2010, Flash Crash, when the Dow Jones Industrial Average plunged about 1000 points—about 9 percent—in an intraday swing. Much of the Flash Crash price volatility was attributed to the role played by computer-driven trading. Over half the trading volume today in the U.S. stock markets is driven by high-frequency trading (HFT) computers.

- A variety of rogue traders who incurred huge losses at firms such as J.P. Morgan ($5.6 billion lost in April and May 2012), UBS ($2 billion lost in September 2011 by Kweku Adoboli), Long-Term Capital Management ($4.6 billion lost in summer 1997), Société Générale (Jérôme Kerviel; $7.2 billion lost in January 2008), and Morgan Stanley (Howie Hubler $9 billion lost, 2007), among others, have demonstrated how fast money can disappear.
- A variety of insider trading scandals involving Raj Rajaratnam, Mitchel Guttenberg, David Tavdy, Eric Franklin, and Sam and Charles Wyly.
- The Facebook (FB) IPO, in which institutions were told in advance about lowered earnings prospects for FB while individuals were given full allocations on an IPO that dropped by more than 50 percent in the first several months of trading.
- The Libor (London Interbank Offered Rate) scandal involving big multinational banks colluding to falsely inflate or deflate this widely used interest rate to profit from trades and give the impression that they were more creditworthy than they actually were.

Clearly, investors have good reason to worry about the stability and integrity of the stock market.

Confidence in Stocks Takeaways. The reality is these events are generally inconsequential relative to the overall size of the market. The world's stock markets are estimated to be worth nearly $40 to $50 trillion. The size of the U.S. stock market is roughly $15 trillion. There is no question that some of these events caused meaningful disruptions in stock market pricing, but history shows they are washed out over time.

Although the events of the last decade look unusual, they are not overwhelmingly unusual. The entire twentieth century was filled with major stock market scandals and disruptions, including two world wars, the Cold War, and Vietnam. Michael Milken, the junk bond king, along with Ivan Boesky and Dennis Levine, did a pretty good job of rattling the financial markets with insider trading and market manipulation activities in the late 1980s.

Because of the vastly increased size of the financial markets, the issues affecting investor confidence today are actually relatively benign compared with the market of 100 years ago. In the early days of the stock market in the late 1800s, investors such as Jay Gould, James Fisk, Russell Sage, Edward Henry Harriman, and J. P. Morgan turned the fledgling stock market into their personal playground. Because the volume of stock trading was relatively small compared with the wealth of these traders, there was ample opportunity to manipulate stock prices.

Until the 1920s, most market fraud affected only the few Americans who were investing. When it was confined largely to battles between wealthy manipulators, the government felt no need to step in. After World War I, however, average Americans discovered the stock market. To take advantage of the influx of eager new money, manipulators teamed up to create stock pools. The pooled funds were used to manipulate prices. The stock pools became very powerful, manipulating even large cap stocks such as Chrysler, RCA, and Standard Oil.

When the stock market collapsed in 1929, both the general public and the government were staggered by the level of corruption that had contributed to the financial catastrophe. Stock pools took the lion's share of the blame, leading to the creation of the Securities and Exchange Commission (SEC) in 1934.

The establishment of the SEC did not end all stock market catastrophes going forward. However, it did represent a major step forward by creating a more level playing field for all stock market participants. The stock market is a living, breathing thing that should be thought of as a work in progress. It is almost certain that the U.S. stock market will never be a perfect place. Yet with all its faults, stocks can be one of the best major investment sectors to achieve attractive risk-adjusted returns and has probably never been as fair as it is today in terms of transparency and efficiency.

CHAPTER SIX

The Story of Modern Finance Theory

THE STORY of modern financial theory is centered on an ongoing argument about whether future stock prices are predictable. Although much of the institutional investment industry has concluded that prices are predictable, academic theory has concluded for the most part that it is impossible to predict future prices unless you have privileged information or some way to manipulate stock prices. The reason this argument is important is that it determines how you should invest in your stock portfolio.

If prices are predictable, you will want to use the services of an active manager to invest in a portfolio of stocks that will outperform the overall market. Rather than worry about fees, you should focus on the value added by the active manager and compare that value to the value added by other available managers and the overall market performance. Paying for performance makes sense if there is performance.

If stock prices are not predictable, you should buy the broad market and passively hold the market portfolio of stocks. The reason you buy and hold is that you believe that future stock prices are, for all practical purposes, random, and that average expected stock returns make the risk/reward trade-off generally attractive. You have to be in the market all the time to catch the important times when the market rallies higher. Because you are a buy-and-hold investor in the market basket of stocks, your primary concern should be fees because fees are the single most important cause of potential portfolio underperformance.

If you believe in the buy-and-hold investment methodology, you are making four important assumptions:

1. Stocks will provide equal or better returns than other asset classes on a risk-adjusted basis. In other words, the expected future returns of the stock market warrant your investment dollars.
2. Stock prices are random and unpredictable.
3. Catching the best appreciation days in the market is worth the expense of catching the worst depreciation days in the market. Gains and losses should be considered as symmetric risks as long as the general trend has a positive slope.
4. Significant downside market volatility will not coincide with a time when you need to withdraw funds from your stock investments.

In 1974, John Bogle started the Vanguard Group, which offered retail investors low-cost, low-turnover funds, including the Vanguard 500 Index, which tracked the S&P 500. Bogle was simply making available to retail customers an actionable way to implement the academic theories of economists such as Eugene Fama, Burton Malkiel, and Paul Samuelson, who argue that buy and hold is the best strategy for stock investing.

Vanguard funds work well for fee-focused buy-and-hold investors. For the most part, they are low-cost funds that passively track large groups of stocks. If the world uniformly believed the academic theory driving a buy-and-hold conclusion, Vanguard and other fund families like it would hold the vast majority of mutual fund assets. However, two of the largest fund companies—PIMCO and Fidelity—are predominantly focused on active management. Many of the fastest-growing segments of the investment industry, including hedge funds, are in active management. Investors are willing to pay higher fees for active management despite the theory that buy and hold is best. The question is why. The durable, long-term answer is outperformance.

The world is changing. Because the U.S. stock market has not appreciated for 12 years, investors are asking for more from their money managers. The Japanese stock market has languished for roughly 30 years. The developed world economies are saddled with high debt levels that could suppress economic growth and equity market appreciation for years to come. It is during the difficult times that investors tend to question the assumptions more rigorously. Investors want results and do not want to suffer through major drawdowns like what was experienced in the Nasdaq collapse or the credit crisis. The good news is that the difficulties of the last decade are a catalyst to drive the investment industry to find a better way.

a. Investing 101

Investing boils down to putting your money to work collecting a return that compensates you for the time value of your money and the risks specific to your particular investment.

Asset pricing theory is about explaining how asset prices are a function of risk. Risk is broken into two key components: time and uncertainty. When you make an investment, you are taking an action on the basis of your expectations about future events. You are making assumptions about the likelihood of future payouts and discounting those expected payouts back to today's prices.

The future is basically a risky place. No one knows what will happen with certainty. The farther forward you forecast, the wider is the array of outcomes that become possible. In other words, as time extends, risk rises. As time extends, you should ask for a higher return to take on the additional risk. The basic idea is that the value of a security today is related to the timing and probability of possible future payouts.

At the time of this writing, you would receive less than a 2 percent annual interest payment on a 10-year loan made to the U.S. government. This is an indication of how low investors' return expectations are across the spectrum of possible investments. Figure 6.1 shows a chart of various interest rates. The difference between the Treasury

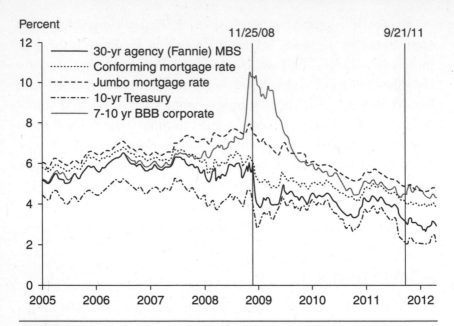

FIGURE 6.1 Yields of Various Debt Securities from 2005 to 2012

Source: Federal Reserve Bank of San Francisco, May 21, 2012.

(risk-free) rate and other, more risky rates is called the spread. How wide or narrow the yield spread is between various risk assets is often used as a measure of risk-on/risk-off. Wide spreads indicate that investors are risk-averse and require a higher rate of return before they will commit money to risky investments. Narrow spreads indicate rising investor comfort with risk.

Simple Investment Example. To make the concept of investing clear, we start by using an example involving a single project with a fairly clear return and risk set. Purely for purposes of explanation, we use an example of an investor who is considering building an apartment building. The project is a go if the financing can be arranged at a reasonable cost and if the building is expected to attract a sufficient number of renters within a reasonable period paying a sufficient amount of rent to compensate the investor for the cost of capital and the project-specific risks.

Although many investors are predominantly focused on the real estate aspects of the deal, including obtaining the building permits, building the apartments, attracting tenants, and collecting rent, the cost and availability of capital is a critical element. If money is readily available at a low price, the number of attractive apartment building projects should increase and vice versa. Much of the time, investments fail not because of poor building quality or an inability to attract customers but because the financial structure of the project was wrong to start with. Ratios of debt to equity and mating the duration of the financing with the duration of the project are beyond the scope of this book. Suffice it to say that debt coverage ratios should be strong and the debt payback terms should roughly match the project payout expectations. The capital structure of the project is worth keeping in the back of your mind as you evaluate investments.

Buying a stock in principle is not much different from deciding to build an apartment building. If you are rational and profit-seeking, you are measuring your capital outlay (purchase cost) against some measure of future returns. In stocks, these returns are often described as dividends and earnings. If the project or stock seems risky, you will demand a high rate of expected return before making the up-front investment. If the project or stock seems like a sure thing, you may be willing to take a lower expected return.

This logic seems straightforward. Unfortunately, it does not come close to capturing the complexities of stock market investing. If this is your model, using price/earnings (P/E) ratios or evaluating a stock price relative to its future expected stream of payouts, you need a better model. If P/E is your primary metric, the beatings will continue until morale improves.

The difference in complexity between project investing and stock market investing is like understanding the circulation pattern in your cup of tea as you stir in the sugar compared with understanding all the currents in all the oceans in the world and their localized impact on weather conditions.

b. History of Financial Theory

Paul Samuelson, a Nobel Prize–winning economist best known for his work on efficient markets and random stock price action, asked Harvard's endowment managers what the secret is to their investment success. Samuelson was told there are two rules for running the Harvard endowment: "1. Never consult the economics department. 2. Never consult the business school" (*An Enjoyable Life Puzzling over Modern Finance Theory*, Paul A. Samuelson, MIT, 2009). The following section lays out the major components of modern finance theory as it is taught to MBAs by guys from the economics department. Understanding where the theory has taken you as an investor and why you might want to step out of the box is fundamental to learning to benefit from this book.

Major Milestones

1900	Louis Bachelier: dissertation, "The Theory of Speculation." Prices fluctuate randomly, and so it is impossible to make mathematical predictions of future prices.
1933	Alfred Cowles: "Can Stock Market Forecasters Forecast?" *Econometrica*, vol.1, 309–324, July 1933. After examining thousands of stock selections made by investment professionals, Cowles found no evidence of an ability to outguess the market.
1938	John Burr Williams: *The Theory of Investment Value* (Amsterdam: North-Holland Publishing Company, 1964). Williams talked about dividends as a determinant of stock value in an early version of the dividend discount model.
1934–1949	Benjamin Graham: *Security Analysis* (1934) and *The Intelligent Investor* (1949). Graham preached selective value investing. Warren Buffett extended the Graham approach by looking at both value and growth. Benjamin Graham and Warren Buffett are not academics and do not necessarily fit in this timeline in two important

ways: (1) Their work is based on active investing rather than theory and (2) they were long-term stockholders after opportunistically buying stocks that had become deeply undervalued (market timing), not buy-and-hold cult members. The reason they are included is that they have had a powerful influence on the investment industry.

1952 Harry Markowitz: "Portfolio Selection," *Journal of Finance*, vol. 7, 77–91, March 952. Markowitz talked about the principle of diversification, which posits that by holding many stocks rather than just a few, an investor can reduce risk while maintaining the same overall expected return.

1964 William F. Sharpe: "Capital Asset Prices: A Theory of Market Equilibrium Under Conditions of Risk," *Journal of Finance*, vol. 19, 425–442, September 1964. Sharpe proposed the capital asset pricing model (CAPM). The CAPM states that investors should invest in the market portfolio, holding a portfolio consisting of all existing securities in proportion to their market capitalization. The idea is that investors are compensated for taking necessary risks (overall market risk) but not for taking unnecessary risk (specific stock risk). Sharpe concluded that market risk is inescapable. Investors whose portfolios differ from the market are playing a zero-sum game, meaning they have taken on additional risk for no additional expected return. Sharpe's work is a cornerstone of passive buy-and-hold investing in the market portfolio. The combination of Markowitz's study of diversification and Sharpe's CAPM produced the retail industry standard method of investing today. The underlying idea is that by holding a group of stocks in a portfolio, one can eliminate the company-specific risk, leaving only the market-related risk. Stock performance directly linked to market movement rather than company-specific drivers is called beta (β). Diversification theoretically made it possible for an investor to have a portfolio of the desired risk level with respect to the market and with a higher expected return than the expected return on any individual stock.

1965   Paul Samuelson: "Proof That Properly Anticipated Prices Fluctuate Randomly," *Industrial Management Review*, vol. 6, 41–49, 1965. Samuelson amplified the argument that stock prices cannot be forecasted if they are properly anticipated in an efficient market in which all known information is priced into equities by rational investors. Samuelson's work added to the body of evidence suggesting that future stock prices are not generally predictable, leading to the idea that owning the market is a better solution than trying to pick stocks. Again, because it is argued that prices are random, investors are advised to buy and hold because they will not be able to anticipate times of market appreciation.

1968   Michael Jensen: "The Performance of Mutual Funds in the Period of 1945–1964," *Journal of Finance*, vol. 23, 389–416, May 1968. Jensen showed that during this period in the market's history, actively managed U.S. mutual funds failed to perform better than a broad market index. He set the precedent for denoting excess performance derived from the actions of an active manager with the symbol alpha (α). Jensen's work added more weight to the passive investment thesis of buy and hold.

1970 +   Economic theory up to this point essentially laid the groundwork for the way the retail investment industry operates today. Investors are advised to allocate their assets between bonds and stocks in accordance with their appetite for risk. In the stock portion of their allocation, investors generally are guided to buy and hold a portfolio representative of the overall stock market.

Fama, Black, Scholes, Merton, Ross, French, Grinod, Kahn, and others have essentially been refining the earlier work. The efficient market hypothesis has been segmented into weak-form efficiency, semistrong-form efficiency, and strong-form efficiency with modestly differing conclusions. The Black-Scholes options pricing formula and arbitrage pricing theory (APT) look at how arbitrage eliminates opportunities for excess returns for no extra risk. Single-factor models explaining stock returns have been replaced by multifactor models.

The net effect of this theory progression is that retail investors are often subjected to major losses and poor portfolio performance during the investment periods that matter to them.

In sharp contrast to retail investing, the institutional world is involved in an ever-increasing amount of quantitative, active, dynamic portfolio management with better risk controls and expected returns than what the theory would say is possible and what retail investors are offered.

c. Random and Efficient

The concept of randomness was most notably applied to the stock market by Paul Samuelson (Nobel Prize in 1970), who published an article in 1965 titled "Proof That Properly Anticipated Prices Fluctuate Randomly." The random walk hypothesis is the idea that future stock prices cannot be anticipated in a market that fully incorporates the expectations and information of all market participants. Efficient markets, the theory goes, incorporate all known information into market prices very quickly, eliminating significant, consistent profit opportunities.

Today, millions of investors are digitally transmitting information near the speed of light to buy and sell stocks collectively in huge volumes. Where the market clears (the point at which buyers and sellers agree to a price and are willing and able to trade) is the market price. Efficient markets theory says this price generally reflects all publicly available information about an asset. As both the speed at which information travels and the speed with which investors can execute their trades increase, the markets become more efficient.

When we first got into the business, institutional trades were taken by phone, filled out on a paper ticket, and run out onto the trading floor. Each order had "spin." Just as when you order a pizza and want a little extra cheese or some red peppers added, orders almost always had a trader's special request added.

Favored customers' orders were handled first. Lower-priority customers were placed at the back of the line and got less attention from the trader. Small guys had to accept bad execution much of the time as the big guys demanded the best order execution. The big guys paid the bills and bonuses. Even though orders were time stamped, traders often traded in a Wild West environment as there were so few electronic systems tracking the activity behind the scenes.

The old paper system was chaotic and slow. It allowed for information to be priced into markets at a rate that human analog sensory systems could deal with. You could pick up the phone, call a client with breaking news, and take and execute the client's order before a stock moved. In fact, you could do this about five times, with each call being made through speed dialers and the calls lasting only a few seconds.

At about the start of the twenty-first century, the markets were digitized. Humans have been replaced with zeros and ones traveling through fiber-optic cables. The American financial sector is one of the largest buyers of technology in the world. It loves the most expensive and fastest gear. Order entry systems work mostly through computers. There is no more spin and touch. Human traders are measured against VWAP (volume-weighted average price) and other computerized trading algorithms.

Today, supercomputers colocated on the exchange floors price information into markets through fiber-optic cables over distances measured in feet. The colocation makes the pipe connecting the computer to the market shorter, decreasing the time for light to travel from A to B. This has made markets "hyperefficient" in terms of pricing information into stocks. It has also made the market more efficient in the sense that it costs less to trade than it used to. The person has been replaced by the machine. Computers have contributed to increased trading volumes (liquidity). According to the *New York Times*, computerized high-frequency trading (HFT) has cut the cost of trading in half since 2000.

Because the market already incorporates all information, there is no point seeking an edge through superior research or analysis. Performing this work, so the theory goes, would increase your investment costs and lower your expected returns. Your expected returns are the market returns minus any costs you incur to obtain those returns.

Although the efficient markets hypothesis dictates that generally excess profit cannot be earned consistently over time, it does allow that a competitive advantage such as superior information (insider trading) and/or superior technology (faster trade execution through better computers, which led to statistical arbitrage and high-frequency trading) can lead to consistently better returns. This book is not about having you use a faster computer or gaining advantaged information about stocks. What we are about is showing you how to earn superior long-term investment returns through disciplined active investment management.

An economist is walking down the street with a friend when he observes a $100 bill lying on the ground. The friend reaches down to pick it up, and the economist says, "Don't bother; if it were a real $100 bill, someone would have already picked it up." This joke captures the spirit of how the market efficiency hypothesis can arrive at a ridiculous conclusion. It also indicates that a strong belief in random prices and efficient markets leaves dollars to be picked up by those observing what is rather than what should be.

It should now be evident that describing market pricing as purely random and efficient is a stretch. What is important about the random walk and efficient market theories is that they have a useful role to play in explaining aggregate stock market movement:

1. Efficient pricing is generally a good way to think about stock prices. Because stocks reflect what active market participants are thinking, stock prices carry a lot of good information. All technical (chart) stock analysis is based on this idea. However, this does not necessarily mean that efficient market prices are an accurate reflection of what will actually happen in the real world in the near term. It is often the case that the world behaves in a manner that is unanticipated by current market prices.

2. The efficient market hypothesis should increase one's confidence in the markets. If you decide that stock prices are tied to underlying fundamental economic activity over time to a material extent rather than being a function of manipulation by institutions and insiders, that is a good thing. Because we believe that stocks are tied to economic activity and perceptions of future economic activity, we participate in the market.

3. Arguing about the degree to which markets are efficient is not a useful exercise when it comes to making money in stocks. They are efficient enough to have a foundation in fundamentals and inefficient enough to make future stock prices somewhat predictable. There are clearly cases in which there is price manipulation or market structural issues that create inefficient pricing. From our standpoint, it is useful to be aware that these situations are a possible explanation of current market conditions as they may affect decisions about short-term trading. Generally, however, they do not dissuade us from looking at the stock market as a fair place to invest.

d. Normal Distribution

Random and efficient is not a perfect way to describe securities pricing. However, the concept that lots of information is priced into stocks is useful and can be helpful in understanding aggregate, normalized stock movement.

What is less useful and potentially more damaging in financial theory is the application of a normal distribution to future potential earnings outcomes and the use of this model to forecast an array of probable future stock prices. Profit-maximizing rational investors often use a company's "earnings power" or expected future earnings to determine whether a stock is overvalued or undervalued. With every guess about what might happen in the future, investors are offered an excellent opportunity to get it wrong and lose money.

In explaining the analysis of a series of probabilistic events in the future, statisticians like to show the results in a diagram called a histogram. Flipping a coin 10 times is often used as an example (Figure 6.2). Over 10 coin flips, you could have heads 5 times and tails 5 times. Or you could have 10 heads in a row or any other combination of heads and tails that could occur in 10 flips of the coin. If you repeated this exercise 1 million times, you would create a range of outcomes. Because the chances of a coin landing on heads

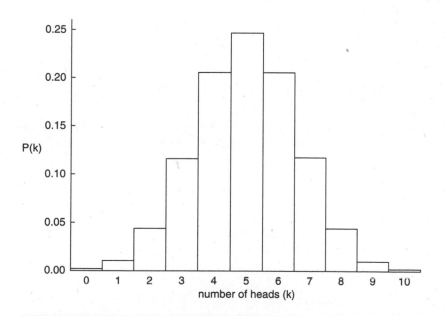

FIGURE 6.2 **Results of Flipping a Coin 10 Times**

or tails is 50/50 and each flip is an independent event, the picture of outcomes called a histogram takes on a normal distribution showing the majority of results falling in line, with the greatest number of outcomes being half heads and half tails.

Coin flipping is an easy way to explain probabilistic testing and charting the results. This histogram has a nice bell shape and is an example of a normal distribution. The y axis shows the probability that a certain number of flips will result in heads. The x axis shows the number of heads out of 10 flips. Almost everyone thinks about coin flipping as producing a 50/50 chance of heads or tails. Hence, it is not much of a surprise that the most likely event in Figure 6.2 is five heads and five tails.

Figure 6.3 shows a normal distribution line graph that essentially smoothes out the chunky bar histogram chart with more observations.

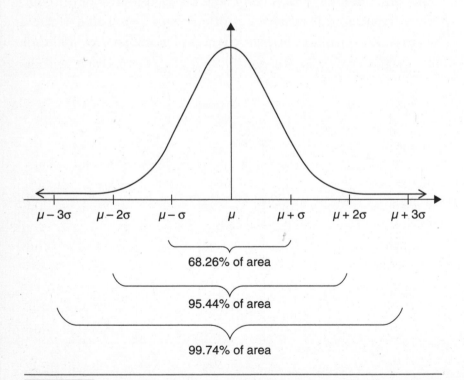

FIGURE 6.3 **Normal Distribution Curve with 1, 2, and 3 Standard Deviations Shown with Probabilities**

The μ symbol in the middle of the x axis stands for the population mean: the average result. The σ symbol is called sigma and represents standard deviation. What the chart is showing is that 68.26 percent of the time what you actually experience will fall within 1 standard deviation of the mean and 95.44 percent of the time actual results will be contained within 2 standard deviations of the mean. Virtually all events (99.74 percent) will be within 3 standard deviations. This is what is meant by a normal distribution.

In looking at the natural world, physics uses a random distribution assumption to explain all kinds of phenomena. A stock market model built on the assumption that stock prices are random has been a less successful application of the random distribution model. There is plenty of research in psychology showing consistent biases inherent in human behavior. Subatomic particles generally do not suffer from human bias. John Maynard Keynes captured this idea in 1936 when he said that most investors' decisions "can only be taken as a result of animal spirits—of a spontaneous urge to action rather than inaction, and not as the outcome of a weighted average of benefits multiplied by quantitative probabilities" (*The General Theory of Employment, Interest and Money*, 1936).

On Thursday, October 8, 1987, Maria went on vacation with her boyfriend. Maria was an options market maker on the Pacific Exchange. Before leaving, she asked her clerk to watch her book. Maria's instructions were not to initiate any new positions and maintain what is called a back-spread position. That means Maria's book was essentially delta-neutral: long stock combined with an equal amount of long put positions or short stock and long calls in an equal amount.

During the week of October 12, 1987, market makers were seeing a tremendous increase in the volume of put buying. When customers buy puts, market makers sell them. They are now short puts, which means they are exposed to losses if stocks decline through the put strike prices. To hedge the position, option market makers will short stock to remain delta-neutral.

In the late 1980s, computerized trading systems were not very sophisticated. Every morning, the market makers would pick up their computer-generated position printouts showing their exposures (net deltas). The Black-Scholes options pricing model that relied on an underlying assumption of a normal distribution gave market makers no reason to expect that an event greater than 3 standard deviations from the mean would ever occur.

On Monday, October 19, 1987, the DJIA dropped by 22.6 percent (508 points). Options volatility (pricing) spiked higher. Market makers who had spent the previous week filling customers' long put orders and who relied on a normal distribution assumption were hammered. Stocks fell way below their put strike prices, and the market makers were not short nearly enough stock to hedge the losses. Black Monday was devastating to those who had assumed a normal distribution. Black Monday is considered a 22-standard-deviation event.

Maria returned from vacation. Her portfolio had been short stock and long puts. Her back-spread account jumped 900 percent higher on Black Monday. About two years later, she dropped her vacation boyfriend and married the clerk who had been watching her book during this time.

In 1994, some of the really smart financial theory guys got together and formed a hedge fund called Long-Term Capital Management (LTCM). Two founding members of the fund, Myron Scholes and Robert C. Merton, shared the 1997 Nobel Prize for Economic Sciences for a new method to determine the value of derivatives (the Black-Scholes model) and are considered thought leaders in finance. Their computer models performed various arbitrage trade strategies to take advantage of the fixed-income arbitrage usually associated with U.S., Japanese, and European bonds. The fund migrated into trading strategies involving merger arbitrage and volatility bets on the S&P 500.

Because of their confidence in a normal distribution of probabilities, they levered up their fund to a ratio of debt to equity of roughly 25 to 1. They also had off-balance-sheet interest rate swap positions with a notional value of roughly $1.25 trillion.

In September 1998, the LTCM fund collapsed. U.S. securities markets were placed under so much strain so that the Federal Reserve Bank of New York was forced to intervene with a multi-billion-dollar bailout to prevent further collapse of the financial markets. The fear was that forced liquidations by LTCM would create a chain reaction of forced selling by other firms that would drive down asset prices in an indiscriminate manner. (This scenario played out for different reasons during the liquidation phase of the 2008–2009 credit crisis, with the Federal Reserve having to provide significant bailout funds to support distressed asset values.)

One of the reasons LTCM collapsed was a failure to recognize the codependency of various scenarios. What LTCM's models had predicted as sure winners became sure losers in an environment where one asset class developed linkages with other events that had not been observed before. When bad things start to happen, the compounding and connectedness of detrimental outcomes can be truly astounding. A series of small problems can all of a sudden create a catastrophic problem that was virtually unimaginable at the outset.

When LTCM went down, Nobel Prize winners Dr. Harry Markowitz (known for the creation of modern portfolio theory) and Dr. Robert Merton said that the Russian currency fluctuations that triggered LTCM's final demise was a "10-sigma"—10 standard deviations away from expected—event. These sigma events have a probability that is best described as zero. As we know from Figure 6.3, 3-sigma events explain 99.74 percent of all occurrences.

For these two Nobel Prize winners to claim that the fund blew up for a reason that never happens makes clear that the experts really did not understand the actual probabilities of possible outcomes. The real world of securities pricing is a complex place that is not captured well with a normal distribution assumption. We should never underestimate the variety of outcomes a complex system can produce. Many of the key assumptions in modern financial theory are based on unknowable volatility parameters.

Paul A. Samuelson in an article titled "An Enjoyable Life Puzzling over Modern Financial Theory" said, "Traders successful over a long time period, in my experience, generally do have a wholesome respect for risk. When things first go against them, their chosen model would say: 'Expected profits will be higher still. However, for canny traders the moment comes when they have to doubt their own model. At that point they close positions and go fishing.'"

Here we have one of the key architects of the buy-and-hold stock ownership cult saying that there are times when getting out entirely is the best course of action, particularly if you are interested in surviving for the long term.

The general partners of LTCM forgot one of the essential rules of trading: always be prepared to be wrong. Whenever a model predicts that something has a negligible chance of failing, the probability that the model can fail should be reviewed carefully. Not getting married to a position is essential to survival.

If the S&P 500 is expected to earn a real return rate of about 7 percent (roughly the long-term average) with a variability of 20 percent, a normal distribution would imply that 68.26 percent of the outcomes will fall in the range centered on +7 percent plus or minus 20 percent—1 standard deviation. It also predicts that 95.44 percent of the outcomes will fall within 2 standard deviations or, in the case of a normally distributed S&P 500 stream of returns over time, −33 percent and +47 percent.

What we find is that the market trading pattern does not fit nicely with a normal distribution. Major sell-offs occur much more frequently than what a normal distribution curve of probabilities would suggest:

- The October 1987 crash was a 21.6-standard-deviation event. Such events are supposed to happen only every 10^{51} years, which is about four times the age of the universe.
- The October 1997 Asian currency crisis should have happened only once every 3 billion years.
- The September 1998 Long-Term Capital Management hedge fund collapse was thought to be possible only once every 10^{21} years.
- In 1987, there were six trading days when the market moved by at least 5 standard deviations from the mean. In 2008, there were 18 such occurrences. Thus, in addition to there being daily return sigma events to worry about, there are clearly high-sigma years to be wary of as well.

Over the last 20 years, we estimate that severe losses occurred about 18 percent of the time, or once every 5 years.

The timing of when a market decides to jump off the ledge is a bit of a mystery, but you know it when you see it. A stock market free fall should be thought of as a time when individual stock attributes do not matter, as there is something so big and bad happening on a macro level that all stocks move in reaction to the threat. One way to measure this is to look at the daily advance/decline reading for the S&P 500. It is rare that this number exceeds 400 in a day, and when it does, the market is usually on a collective run. Between 1990 and 2002, the average number of days when this number was 400 or greater during a year was three. During the trading week of May 28, 2012, we had three readings greater than 400 in a single week.

Major downside market events usually involve panics that are characterized by a rush to liquidate everything. Forced liquidations occur when an investor is required to meet a capital call and usually involve an imbalance between rapidly rising losses/withdrawals (and debt exposure) and a nonappreciating asset base. When panic sets in, most probabilistic models do a poor job of anticipating the severity of the selling. Severe panics usually bring into play factors that are not seen during normal trading periods. This is what makes panic selling so hard to predict. An extensive database used to analyze the distribution of possible future market outcomes may severely underestimate the risk and pressures of panic selling.

You may have heard the term *tail risk*. Tails are the area under the probability curve farthest from the mean. They are the parts of the distribution curve that are expected to have probabilities near zero and that continuously approach zero as you move farther away from the mean result. Fat tails are actual probabilities away from the mean that are farther above the x axis zero line than a normal distribution would imply. What often causes financial investment programs to fall apart is that the probability of a tail event is underestimated. In these cases, tail risk was fat.

Calculating probabilistic outcomes is difficult because it is almost always impossible to know all the factors that affect a possible outcome. Although it runs counter to all of our experience, it is possible to have a coin that flips three tails in a row after every head flip without having a biased coin. At Stanford University, Professor Persi Diaconis proved that a coin will land the same way if flipped with the exact same amount of force on each flip. It turns out that coin flipping does not necessarily fit a normal distribution if a coin is flipped in a certain way. Persi got his start in mathematics by figuring out various methods to prevent getting cheated at the seedy Caribbean casinos he frequented.

Probabilities are not necessarily static. They can be conditional. In other words, probabilities in the real world are often not like flipping a coin and having a 50/50 chance of heads or tails on every flip. In the investment world, one event can change the probabilities of the expected outcome of the next event. Often, we see cascading feedback loops during times of crisis that make a continuation of a downtrend or an uptrend much more likely.

Further complicating predicting probabilities is the ever-changing world. Changing circumstances can skew probabilities to one side or the other over time. As our confidence in predicting the future rises from what we have observed in the past, we could be missing the evolving nature of the underlying probabilities.

Investors often ignore outlier events because the farther you move away from the mean event, the lower the probability of the outlier assuming a normal distribution becomes. Normal distribution tends to breed a certain false comfort that life will generally remain within some acceptable bounds.

If you knew that from January 3, 1950, through July 31, 2012, the average daily return of the S&P 500 was 0.03 percent and the standard deviation was 0.98 percent (Yahoo Finance, CFA Institute), you might conclude that these results are remarkably similar to the mean and standard deviation of the normal distribution of 0 and 1, respectively. The normal distribution description falls apart when the market moves farther away from the mean.

Rather than ignore outlier events and pretend they don't exist, we believe investors should at least consider that fat tails characterize stock market returns and have a plan for avoiding them when they are on the downside. One negative outlier event can wipe out all your cumulative gains.

We have described how a normal distribution assumption does a poor job of accounting for the unexpectedly high number of stock market blowups. Some of the smartest minds in finance have been financially wiped out by not predicting the blowups accurately. There are several important trends that may cause the market to be more susceptible to blowups rather than less so going forward:

- Money is moving at an increasingly rapid pace. Over half of the volume of stocks traded in the U.S. markets today is done by computers conducting high-speed trades in an effort to capture small arbitrage opportunities or small price movements based on computerized analysis. This is called high-frequency trading (HFT). Knight Capital Group (KCG) lost roughly 75 percent of its stock value and $440 million in two days in August 2012 as a result of a bad HFT software implementation. Knight at the time accounted for roughly 11 percent of all HFT clearing.

  Computerized trading programs can accentuate negative market trends. When trades were placed via the open outcry system before the rise of HFT over the last decade, every step had human involvement. Orders were called in by telephone, transcribed by humans, and passed on to others for execution, confirmation, and settlement. At every point, a human could recognize if a major mistake had been made. With HFT trading today, trades go from electronic order entry to execution with little to no human oversight and fewer risk controls. When markets are undergoing a panic or some other out-of-the-box circumstance, computers can speed the pace of the panic. On May 16, 2010, the DJIA dropped by about 9 percent intraday as a result of out-of-control computerized trading in what is called the Flash Crash.

- The danger of dramatic swings in value in U.S. stocks today has been elevated by having world financial markets become more interconnected than ever before. This is particularly true in the financial sector, in which huge multinational banks dominate capital flows. Not too long ago, a Greek default would have been inconsequential to world stock markets. Today, because of Greece's connection with the euro currency, a simple default and write-down of Greek debt has significant consequences for the 17-country euro zone as a whole. With uncertainty in the euro zone, economic activity slows. A slower European economy leads to fewer imports from China and the United States. Additionally, European banks facing potential balance sheet write-downs require higher core capital ratios to protect against a worst-case scenario. U.S. banks with exposure to European sovereign debt and the euro currency also are required to become defensive. The potential consequence of a failure of the Greek economy, an economy smaller than that of the state of Michigan, is a measurable slowdown in global growth and a possible currency and debt crisis.
- Problems in Russia, Greece, Spain, Iceland, Portugal, Ireland, Italy, France, Africa, OPEC, China, Japan, and so on, can spread to our market in minutes. Not only is money moving across borders faster, it is moving between asset classes faster. Hedge funds now have about $2 trillion under management. They can buy and sell virtually any asset class and often do. Hedge funds tend to be aggressive traders and look to gain an advantage by finding arbitrage opportunities across borders and asset classes. In the press, these types of trades are often called *carry trades*. When huge, multi-billion-dollar hedge fund carry trades go poorly (e.g., the Long-Term Capital Management blowup in 1998), the U.S. stock market can suffer a rapid setback.
- The financial industry continues to manufacture increasingly sophisticated derivative-type investment instruments that increase

the leverage of what is traded. Leverage increases potential volatility. Small changes in underlying value have a magnified impact when you apply leverage. When you take leverage from 2:1 to 40:1 to 150:1 (Fannie Mae and Freddie Mac in 2008), get ready for a wild ride. When you add the fact that many of these new investment instruments are not fully understood by the people who trade them and there is poor visibility into the market where these instruments trade, the consequences of the trading can become even more volatile.

As an example of how derivatives can distort expected future values, basic equity options trading activity often invalidates a normal distribution assumption for individual stocks. When options are traded, options market makers often execute trades on a delta-neutral basis. Because options contracts often remain open until expiration, the market maker continuously adjusts his holdings to remain delta-neutral as the underlying stock prices change. In effect, staying delta-neutral often requires an options market maker to buy or sell stock as a hedge against the open options contracts in her book. By staying delta-neutral, the market maker is generally able to capture the options premium, which is a source of profit to the market maker.

This has been called collecting pennies in front of a steamroller. If all goes well, market makers get rich collecting pennies. If risk is not carefully managed, they are flattened by a steamroller that represents the idea that they were not delta-neutral when the underlying stock made a significant, unexpected move. Because market makers have net exposure, they potentially can have all their pennies taken away by a single massive loss. The one major loss sustained by being run over by the steamroller would make the collection of all the pennies over the years irrelevant. By taking a vacation, Maria avoided this exact scenario on Black Monday, October 19, 1987.

Depending on how the open contracts are positioned on a particular stock, changes in the stock price can cause a sudden acceleration in additional price change. For example, if there are a significant

EMC Stock Price : 26.97 on Aug 07 2012 Target Date Aug 17, 2012

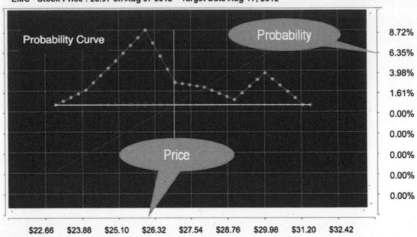

FIGURE 6.4 EMC Pricing Probability Curve Derived from EMC Option Open
Interest for August 7, 2012

number of put contracts open and the stock begins to decline, the
market maker may have to short a large volume of stock to remain
delta-neutral. The market maker's hedging activity can cause
acceleration in the rate of stock price decline. This options acceleration factor often plays a role in explaining how a stock can go on a
sudden streak, either higher or lower, and how events in the market
are often not independent. Figure 6.4 shows a histogram of stock
prices for EMC implied by various open option contracts on August
17, 2012. Because of the high volume of open put positions sold by
market makers (customers long EMC puts) and the high volume of
open call positions bought by market makers (customers short EMC
calls), a small move downward in EMC could stimulate a significant
amount of short selling by market makers, causing an acceleration to
the downside in the stock. Notice that the highest-probability event is
that the stock will trade lower as the probability curve is shifted to the
left of the vertical white line representing the current stock price.

Assuming a normal distribution may be one of the most misleading and dangerous assumptions one can make in finance.

e. Correlation and Modern Portfolio Theory

Correlation is a measure of how one asset moves in relationship to another. Correlation measures range from 1 (perfectly positively correlated) to –1 (perfectly negatively correlated). Assets that move up or down together in lockstep have a correlation of +1. Assets that move in exactly the opposite directions by the same amount have a correlation of –1. Assets that move randomly with no correlation have a correlation of zero.

A cornerstone of gaining asset protection through diversification is correlation. If assets that behave differently—do not have a positive correlation of +1—are combined in a portfolio, the overall volatility of the portfolio can be reduced. If one asset goes up and the other goes down by roughly the same amount and the assets are held in equal amounts, the net effect is no change to the overall portfolio. If the noncorrelated assets have equal expected returns, the target portfolio's expected return can be achieved with less risk.

Harry Markowitz introduced modern portfolio theory (MPT) in an article published in 1952 and updated in 1959, presenting an efficient frontier of optimal investment. MPT is the theory that you can combine a group of diversified assets with different correlations to create a portfolio that has been optimized for maximum expected return for a particular amount of risk. Alternatively, you can set the expected return level to a fixed amount and then use MPT to determine which combination of assets delivers this return for the least amount of risk. Solving the equation for return by using a fixed level of risk places your portfolio on the "efficient frontier." Figure 6.5 shows an example of how the efficient frontier is often presented.

Using correlations effectively in a portfolio for risk management is based on generating reasonably accurately estimates of correlations of different asset classes by analyzing historical returns. Figure 6.6 is a chart of the long-term average annualized volatility and correlations to the S&P 500 of various asset classes. EAFE stands for an index compiled by Morgan Stanley of stocks traded in Europe, Australia, and the Far East. Notice that the S&P 500's correlation to itself is 1.

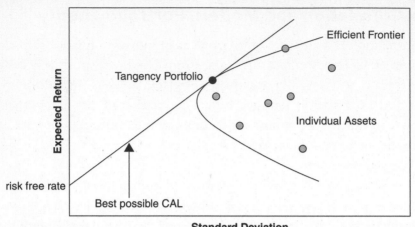

FIGURE 6.5 The Efficient Frontier

Source: Calculated by Rydex SGI using data from Bloomberg.

	Annualized volatility	Correlation to S&P 500
S&P 500	21.4%	1.00
Bonds	4.0%	−0.26
Commodities	25.6%	0.22
7-10 Y Treasuries	6.9%	−0.33
Emerging Markets	21.1%	0.43
EAFE	19.5%	0.46

Source: Calculated by Rydex SGI using data from Bloomberg. Performance displayed is past performance, which is no guarantee of future result. The referenced indices are unmanaged and not available for direct investment. Different time periods would have different results. The index returns do not reflect any management fees, transaction costs or expenses. See appendix for representative index information.

FIGURE 6.6 Long-Term Asset Class Correlation with the S&P 500

Correlations are tricky because they can change over time. They change particularly dramatically during times of crisis. We are not just talking about the correlations between equities—growth and value; large, mid, and small cap; domestic and foreign—but those between equities and bonds and essentially the value of all other dollar-denominated assets in your life.

One-Year Correlation of Returns
(using Vanguard Equity Funds)
calculated 01/07/09

Asset Category	Mutual Fund	Correlation to VFINX	Alternative ETF
S&P 500	VFINX	1.000	SPY
Total US	VTSMX	0.999	VTI
World Ex US	VFWIX	0.940	VEU
EAFE	VDMIX	0.935	VEA
Europe	VEURX	0.925	VGK
Pacific	VPACX	0.910	VPL
Emerging	VEIEX	0.854	VWO

FIGURE 6.7 **Stocks Move Together in Times of Crisis; One-Year Correlation of Various Stock Return Indexes Calculated on January 7, 2009**

Source: www.QVMgroup.com.

Figure 6.7 is a chart of the correlation between various world equity markets and the S&P 500 on January 7, 2009. Remember that a correlation of +1 indicates that two asset classes move exactly in sync in the same direction. As you can see by the numbers being fairly close to 1, diversification during the credit crisis lost almost all of its protective value just when investors needed it most.

Figure 6.8 shows the correlation among U.S. large cap stocks extending back to 1926. Various times of crisis are identified on the chart. These times coincide with rising correlations. It is interesting to note that the European sovereign debt crisis caused correlations to rise to all-time highs in September 2011. The market is increasingly being traded as a group rather than as individual securities. This may be due partly to the increasing use of index and exchange-traded funds (ETFs).

This figure makes it immediately evident that diversifying by owning a basket of stocks to reduce overall portfolio volatility (risk) works well sometimes and not so well at times when stocks

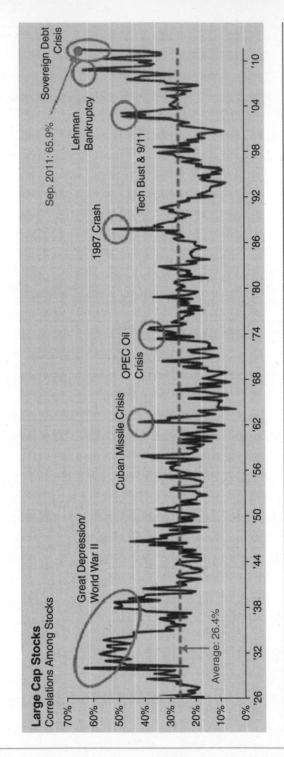

FIGURE 6.8   A Long-Term View of Stock Correlation; Correlation Reaches All-Time High in September 2011

Source: J.P. Morgan Asset Management.

are moving together with high positive correlation. During times of crisis, the benefits of diversification are substantially reduced because correlations among risk assets approach +1.

During a crisis, fear is the predominant emotion. Consumer confidence plunges, and economic activity slows as a result. Not only do stocks move down together as a group because of macro forces, bonds can be negatively affected as a group. During the credit crisis of 2008–2009, corporate bond values collapsed as perceived default risk jumped higher. U.S. Treasuries appreciated because there was a flight to safety. Depending on what types of bonds you held in your portfolio, diversification across bond and stock asset classes might not have offered your portfolio the protection you had anticipated.

Mixing noncorrelated assets in a portfolio is a central idea of risk management in modern finance theory. There is no question that mathematically this is a good idea. The problem is that correlations change over time and often approach 1 at exactly the wrong times.

f. Capital Asset Pricing Model

William F. Sharpe created the CAPM while working on his dissertation as a PhD candidate at the University of California, Los Angeles. He had read "Portfolio Selection" by Markowitz. Although he advocated a diversified portfolio to reduce risk, Markowitz did not provide a way for investors to assess how various holdings operate together, or correlate.

What Sharpe did with the capital asset pricing model (CAPM) was create a straightforward way to think about risk and reward. According to the CAPM, every investment carries two distinct risks. One is the risk of being in the market, which Sharpe calls systematic risk. This risk, later labeled beta, cannot be diversified away. The second risk—unsystematic risk—is specific to a company's fortunes. Since this uncertainty can be mitigated through diversification, the CAPM says that a portfolio's expected return hinges solely on its beta: its relationship to the overall market. The CAPM helps measure portfolio risk and the return an investor can expect for taking that risk.

An important insight of the CAPM is that higher expected returns are tied to a greater risk of doing badly in bad times. In good times, higher beta should mean higher expected returns than the market portfolio. In bad times, this situation is reversed. You can enter estimates of risk/return correlation into a computer and find efficient portfolios. In this way, you can get more return for a particular risk and less risk for a particular return.

Although the CAPM attempts to reduce stock-specific risk, it fails to address the biggest risk of all: the risk of owning equities. There may be times when the best way to manage risk is to reduce your equity exposure to zero. This book is about playing winning runs and avoiding losing runs.

One of the complications of risk management using buy and hold and the principles of CAPM is the term of your investment horizon. As your investment horizon extends, the chances of your being subjected to a major down market rise. Gains and losses are not symmetric. It takes a 100 percent gain to recover from a 50 percent loss. If stock market returns are declining on a secular basis as a result of certain macro economic conditions, including high levels of government debt, the importance of avoiding a major down market becomes even more important. Because our investment time horizons are finite, we run the risk of not having sufficient time to make back what we have lost in a major down market.

In an interview with Jonathan Burton in 1998, William Sharpe was asked, "You've devoted much of your career to the study and understanding of market risk. Are today's investors focused enough on the downside?"

Sharpe replied: "Investment decisions are moving to individuals who are ill-prepared to make them. These are complicated issues. To say, here are 8,000 mutual funds, or even here are 10, do what's right, is not very helpful. The software versions and some of the human versions of the advice that people are getting often seem to ignore risk. They're bookkeeping schemes in which you earn 9 percent every year like clockwork. You die right on schedule. There's no uncertainty at all. Making a decision as to stocks vs. bonds vs. cash and about how much to save, without even acknowledging uncertainty—let alone trying to estimate it—seems to me the height of folly."

MPT, the efficient frontier, and CAPM have formed a straitjacket holding retail investors in stocks through all market conditions. The true test of any hypothesis is time. As time has gone by, the buy-and-hold thesis has not held up well during significant portions of market history.

g. The Market Portfolio

Modern finance theory makes the assumption that capital is free flowing and finds the optimum balance between various stocks and between stocks, bonds, and other investment asset classes. The proportionate holdings of all liquid financial securities are held in optimum ratios as determined by the collective input of all investors. The aggregate investment ratio is called the market portfolio.

Because the market portfolio is presumed to be the market-efficient allocation of capital for an average risk tolerance, the theory suggests that this balance should be your benchmark if not your actual investment allocation. Economists will tell you that the market portfolio represents the consensus expectation about the risk and return of each asset class, taking into account current conditions and future expectations. If you deviate from this allocation balance, the theory proclaims that you are market timing.

There are lots of reasons to believe that capital is not entirely free flowing. As capital flows become more restricted, the argument that the market portfolio is the most efficient portfolio becomes harder to make. In Chapters 8, 9, and 20, we discuss the current state of the mutual fund industry. With style boxes, fee structures, 401(k) investment restrictions, and so on, there are plenty of reasons to believe that the market portfolio is not the result of free flowing capital markets seeking optimization.

The theory points out that if you are overweight or underweight relative to the market portfolio, you reduce your diversification and increase your exposure to economic events that affect the asset classes remaining in your portfolio. By definition, this observation is correct. It also may be the desired outcome.

h. Portfolio Optimization

Modern financial theory has been codified into portfolio optimization software that is used by many of the larger financial institutions. Monte Carlo simulation, a specific form of portfolio optimization, is used by sophisticated financial firms to analyze the probability that an asset today will have a set of specific values in the future. Simulation programs run through computers can test millions of scenarios and provide an array of possible outcomes with probabilities tied to those outcomes.

Monte Carlo analysis is a way to study situations in which the outcomes appear to have the characteristics of random events (stochastic processes). In 1905, Albert Einstein wrote a paper in which he used this type of probabilistic analysis to look at suspended particles in liquid over time. The analysis was used by scientists working on the atomic bomb. Economists have borrowed this type of analysis to explain stock prices.

It involves looking at a potential set of outcomes over time (sample path). For example, if you invest $10,000 in the S&P 500 index, it will give you the probabilities of value over a time period you deem relevant. If you look at outcomes over the period of a few minutes or days, the returns will give more of a sense of the current volatility than of the expected outcome. If you look at it over the period of 100 years, the outcomes will all look fairly close. Monte Carlo is time-dependent. Over short periods, all you are seeing is the volatility. Over longer periods, you are measuring expected return.

Monte Carlo analysis can be used to compare thousands if not millions of potential sample paths. If an investment of $10,000 has an expected value of $15,000 after 10 years but could be $10 or $50,000 during that time, it may not be as attractive to you as a similar investment of $10,000 with the same expected value but a possible range of outcomes of $9,000 to $16,000.

One of the problems with computer modeling and Monte Carlo analysis is that because the analysis uses sophisticated modeling and lots of computer processing power, people can be overconfident about the output. Modeling expected future performance of investments relies heavily on encoding the Monte Carlo simulation software with roughly accurate probabilities for various investment classes to perform in a certain way in response to a wide range of economic conditions. Although computer model outputs tend to look impressive and carry a sense of exactitude, garbage in usually means garbage out.

You may be wondering why major money management firms using sophisticated modern financial theory combined with computer-calculated optimization are doing so poorly. The California Public Employees' Retirement System with roughly $233 billion under management made a 1 percent return for the fiscal year ending June 30, 2012. That 1 percent rate of return didn't come close to its 7.5 percent target rate of return. Theory would say that this outcome fits within the bounds of expected outcomes. The only difficulty is that underperformance has been a chronic condition rather than a one-time event. Actual performance over time suggests that erroneous inputs into simulation models have inflated return expectations.

i. Conclusions

The primary conclusion of modern financial economic theory is that the optimum stock ownership strategy is buy and hold. In a perfectly efficient market, future prices are simply random deviations from the current price. All pertinent information is reflected in current valuations at any specific time. Because stock prices are not predictable, there is no good way to time when to buy and sell in a repeatable manner that will consistently outperform a buy-and-hold strategy. If the market declines, investors just need to be patient, as prices always come back. So far, this last statement when viewed over the past 115 years has been mostly true (the Nasdaq has yet to return to its all-time high reached in 2000), but unfortunately not in a time frame that fits with our lives.

When you buy and hold, you should buy and hold securities in exactly the same ratios as the market holds the securities. For example, if Apple is the largest stock in the market and represents a disproportionate share of investment dollars relative to an equal weighting of all stocks, you should exactly match the market weightings.

Although we did not directly discuss the impact of fees in this section, a buy-and-hold strategy that imitates the market portfolio relies on keeping fees low. Your performance relative to the market will be increasingly diminished as fees go higher since the strategy boils down to market return minus fees. We will have a lot more to say about this in Chapter 20, but fees are an important consideration if you are a passive investor.

We suspect that if you have followed the buy-and-hold path over the last 12 years, you are highly disappointed with your investment results. Buying and holding stocks since the start of the twenty-first century has offered less than long-term average returns to date. The S&P 500 is down in inflation-adjusted and absolute returns for the first 12 years of the century. The date when you will have to start taking money from your savings to pay for retirement or some other major expenditure is now 12 years closer.

In 1998, Wharton professor Jeremy Siegel published a bestselling book called *Stocks for the Long Run* in which he argued that the 6.6 percent average annual gain stocks had averaged from 1912 through 1998 was a "constant" rate of return that investors could rely on. He made the case that over almost any 10-year period, stocks will produce better investment returns than will the alternatives.

Siegel's book was released at the end of a tremendous bull run that extended from 1982 to 2000. In the wake of such a powerful advance, no one doubted his statement about a steady 6.6 percent real return from equities. In fact, many individual investors believed that stock market returns were going to continue at about a 12 percent to 14 percent annual pace. With stocks booming and interest by the investment public in equities near all-time highs, Siegel's investment book quickly became one of the bestselling finance books ever.

His timing as an author could not have been better. The thousands of readers who bought the book for investment purposes could not have timed it any more poorly. By the end of 2012, if you compared the return of stocks for the past 10, 20, and 30 years with that of long-term Treasury bonds, you would find that the bonds outperformed the broad stock market. The reality of the world is that higher-risk stocks do not always reward investors with excess return.

In 2012, Bill Gross, the billionaire cofounder of PIMCO, the largest bond management firm in the world, argued in his August 2012 investor newsletter that stock investors should expect to receive long-term returns substantially less than 6.6 percent. Gross compared people's blind faith in an average annual real return of 6.6 percent from equities with being a member of a cult, specifically the "cult of equity." Gross stated: "If wealth or real GDP was only being created at an annual rate of 3.5 percent over the same period of time (1912–1998), then somehow stockholders must be skimming 3 percent off the top each and every year. If an economy's GDP could only provide 3.5 percent more goods and services per year, then how could one segment (stockholders) so consistently profit at the expense of the others (lenders, laborers and government)?"

He went on to answer his own question by saying that part of the excess gain made by stockholders came at the expense of workers who experienced declining real labor rates for 40 years since the 1970s. As Gross said, "labor gaveth, capital tooketh away." Much of the secular decline in labor rates was due to the globalization of the labor market and outsourcing of jobs to cheaper labor markets around the world. The government also made a contribution to shareholders as corporate tax rates are now at 30-year lows.

Gross makes the mathematical point that 6.6 percent average annual stock returns cannot continue indefinitely: "If stocks continue to appreciate at a 3 percent higher rate than the economy itself (assumed to be about 3.5 percent average long-term GDP growth), then stockholders will command not only a disproportionate share of wealth but nearly all of the money in the world! Owners of 'shares' using the rather simple 'rule of 72' would double their advantage every 24 years and in another century's time would have 16 times as much as the skeptics who decided to skip class and play hooky from the stock market."

Dr. Mohamed A. El-Erian, CEO and co-CIO of PIMCO, provided further clarification of Gross's comments regarding the "cult of equity dying" before the market open on August 21, 2012, during an interview on CNBC. Dr. El-Erian said that important takeaways from Bill's observations are the following:

- Equity investors will have to be much more agile to capture equity returns going forward. Buy-and-hold strategies will disappoint if one expects to see returns equivalent to what was captured from 1912 to 1998.
- Equity investors will have to use better risk management. Major losses will be harder to make back in a more slowly appreciating stock market.
- Equity investors should look for strategies that create alpha. Alpha is essentially return created by actions taken by a money manager that are in excess of the market return.

By connecting the dots and stating that investors should look for strategies that create alpha, Dr. El-Erian is clearly stating that it is a misconception that efficient markets cannot be predictable. The reality is that markets can be both predictable and efficient. The key is recognizing that investor risk premiums vary. If one understands the relationship between risk premiums and stock values, it is possible to employ tactical asset allocation strategies to improve investment returns.

The Nobel Prize–winning economist Paul Samuelson, reflecting on modern finance theory, said: "I learned to carefully abstain from influencing successful traders by offering them my macroeconomic views. Most of such views were registered already in yesterday's and today's markets. Star traders—such as Bruce Kovner and Paul Tudor Jones—somehow had the knack to go beyond what was already in today's financial pages. To maintain their positive alphas required a concentration that for me had to be devoted to *avant garde* scientific economic discoveries."

James Simon of the Renaissance Technologies (a multi-billion-dollar hedge fund engaging in short-term quantitative trading, charging fees up to 5 percent on assets and 44 percent of profits) must laugh daily at the idea that stock prices are not predictable. Since 1989, the firm's $5 billion Medallion Fund has averaged 35 percent annual returns after fees. The Goldman Sachs high-speed computer trading group also makes a mockery of modern finance theory. So do Warren Buffett and the managers of the Harvard, Yale, Princeton, and Stanford endowments.

In this book, we are going to ask you to think differently from the crowd. We are going to show you where the crowd may not have considered all the possible influences fully and may have arrived at erroneous conclusions as a result.

If you have made it this far, you have passed through the most challenging part of the book. From here on, we begin to talk about real-world events and concrete ways to recognize and participate in winning streaks and avoid losing streaks.

CHAPTER SEVEN

The Story of Mike

Mike learned all he needed to know during the first third of his life but waited until the last third to put it to work. Mike was born in Pittsburgh, the son of a truck driver. His father founded a small trucking company with his brother. Both drove trucks, with Mike's father serving as the company's brains and his uncle as the brawn.

Right out of the gate this might sound like just another run-of-the-mill story about a son of a trucker born in Pittsburgh making it big on Wall Street, but it is not. Mike's trucking dad did not fit the stereotype. Rather than having an overriding interest in some of the more immediate pleasures in life, Mike's father loved stocks. He preached stocks. And he enjoyed the benefits of running a profitable trucking company, including membership at the local golf country club. He spent his idle hours imbuing Mike with a strong appreciation of the joys of stock investing and golf.

Mike spent almost all his idle time growing up on the golf course or playing gin rummy in the clubhouse. In some ways, Mike's early life was much like Sonny's except that Sonny's tennis and backgammon were Mike's golf and gin rummy. Like Sonny, Mike got good at both his sport and his betting discipline early on. By the mid-1950s, when Mike was just reaching double-digit birthdays, he was playing gin with anyone he could find and always for money. As Mike says, you don't play gin rummy unless dollars are at stake. The same was true on the golf course. By age 12, Mike had saved enough money from his card and golf winnings to open a bank account. More important, he was developing a sharpened sense for numbers and betting.

When Mike asked his father for help opening a bank account, his trucker dad advised him not to bother with the bank but to buy stocks. After the early 1930s depths of the market decline during the Great Depression, stocks had been working their way higher. Although the market did not reach its 1929 high until 1954, for those who had bought on or after 1933, the stock market had been a friendly place. As Mike continued to hone his golf and gin rummy skills during the late 1950s and early 1960s, stocks kept trending higher.

Mike's first stock was AT&T because it had a higher dividend yield than the interest being offered by the bank. AT&T also had a history of raising dividends. Mike had learned from the stock sermons of his father that he should invest in stocks that offered safety of principal, yield, and possible growth. AT&T fit the bill.

As Mike approached high school, his winnings at the gin table and on the golf course began to migrate from hundreds of dollars to thousands of dollars. His next stock was White Motor, a truck manufacturer that lasted from 1900 to 1980. By the time Mike graduated from Ohio University in 1965, White Motor had tripled and AT&T had quadrupled. Mike was hooked. All he wanted to do was be in the stock market. In the mid-1960s, however, Mike thought the only people who worked on Wall Street came into the business already rich and had a lot of rich friends willing to become instant customers. Mike focused his studies on accounting as the next best thing.

In the mid-1960s, the Pittsburgh-based municipal bond house Singer, Dean & Scribner was looking to hire municipal bond salespeople. They came to Ohio University and made it clear that they were willing to hire people like Mike. For Mike, it was as if a hidden path to his dreams had suddenly become illuminated. Singer, Dean & Scribner was showing that a guy like Mike, the son of a stock-preaching, golf-junkie trucker, could work on Wall Street. Unfortunately for Mike, Wall Street would have to wait as the Vietnam draft was calling.

After returning from his tour of duty in the Army, Mike finally landed his first Wall Street job with Blyth & Co. at 19 Wall—New Yorkers drop the "Street." Blyth was willing to have Mike train for a year in the back office for $450 per month. Mike's love affair with stocks made him willing to do anything to get close to the action. He saw the opportunity at Blyth as the equivalent to getting a master's degree in finance.

At the time, Blyth & Co. was the largest trading firm on Wall Street. Traders were afraid to go to the bathroom. They were afraid to leave their desks for fear that someone would come in and hit their bid or take their offer. For the 1960s, the action was fast and furious. The firm was so busy that it paid no attention to the trainees in the back room.

In 1965, according to the U.S. Department of Commerce, Bureau of the Census, the average (median) American household annual income was $6,900. In 1965, Mike watched a Blyth broker named Roger buy 10,000 shares of a stock for $4 per share. The stock ran to $180 for a paper gain of $1,760,000. Mike was mentally ruined. Real work made no sense to Mike relative to the work of Wall Street. The hook was set deep.

Sitting in the back room of Blyth in New York ceased being a learning exercise almost immediately. Mike needed to get his hands directly into the action. Within a year, he moved back to Pittsburgh, where Blyth maintained an office to service Mellon Bank. In the Pittsburgh office, Mike was allowed to come out of the back room and pursue his own accounts and conduct his own trading. Over the next two and a half years, he opened more accounts than anyone else at the firm.

Business at Blyth was good, but once again, as happens frequently on Wall Street, Mike's career had stalled. Wall Street does not spend a lot of time worrying about employee development. Senior members of Wall Street firms are scrambling as fast as they can to enrich themselves. If the junior guys can't figure out how to get a piece of the action on their own, they are unfit for Wall Street. In Mike's case, he was working under a guy who knew just one stock, Nalco Chemical. It was time to move back to the heart of the action in New York City and play a bigger game.

The investment banking and brokerage firm of Hornblower & Weeks was willing to give Mike six months to sink or swim. Survival of the fittest is how Wall Street keeps its edge. He had interviewed at Lehman Brothers, but the guy who ran the Lehman office looked like he might be difficult to work for, and Mike thought that getting six months, let alone six weeks, was a stretch. It was 1969, and Mike still had not made real money, especially by Wall Street standards.

Once back in New York, Mike needed to add the familiarity and pleasures of golf and gin rummy to his life to feel whole. He joined the first golf club that would let him in, the Rockland Country Club. It was there that he met a *Newsweek* ad salesman who informed him that the Winged Foot Golf Club was looking for young new members who could play golf well. Mike scraped together the $2,500 entrance fee and joined.

Through his play on the golf course, Mike formed critical business relationships. He met a man named McKenzie who made fasteners. McKenzie told Mike he already had eight brokers. Mike said that what McKenzie needed was not another broker but a money manager. McKenzie eventually gave Hornblower's money management group $1 million to manage.

Things were beginning to heat up for Mike. His pay and influence as a broker were on the rise. As many guys who are new to Wall Street do, Mike was feeling an urgency to grow his business at an increasingly fast pace. It was time to move again. It was 1973. This time, Mike went on to Newhard Cook & Co. Inc., where he was given every account east of the Mississippi. Newhard Cook's headquarters were on the western bank of the Mississippi in St. Louis, Missouri.

Mike moved from Hornblower to Newhard along with fellow broker Howard Hebert. Hebert had been working on a market timing service since 1971. Hebert was also fascinated with high relative strength stocks and began to use computers to compile relative strength statistics on roughly 4,000 stocks. In 1973, he shared his system with Mike.

What Hebert showed Mike was the power of owning high relative strength stocks in bullish markets. Mike, whose brain was already addicted to the adrenaline rush of fast stock profits, found the turbocharging of results with high relative strength stocks to be even more addictive. Hebert's relative strength system gave Mike a disciplined way to judge the future prospects of 4,000 stocks. It also provided a moving average crossover (MAC) model to judge the overall health of the market as either bullish or bearish. Moving average crossover models are one of the longest-standing and most successful market timing systems. Because it mattered to his financial success, Mike paid careful attention to both the MAC model and high relative strength stocks. In the game of Wall Street, having an opinion—buy or sell—is essential to generating commissions. Being right more than wrong builds a career.

At the same time, Mike was forming a lasting friendship on the golf course with George Chestnutt, one of the most successful portfolio managers of that era and in charge of the American Investors Fund for 30 years. According to *Financial World* magazine, the fund's return from January 16, 1958 (inception), through March 31, 1964, was 160.5 percent versus the Dow Jones Industrial Average return of 82.67 percent.

Many consider George Chestnutt the father of relative strength. He was a chemical engineer from the University of Montana who would calculate the slope of stock curves on the basis of 20 separate segments to derive a relative strength ranking on 1,000 stocks. The more current portions of the stock's price history were assigned a higher weighting than was older price performance. After comparing the price performance of each stock against the group over time, he would then order stocks by their relative price strength compared with the overall group. He would personally punch the computer cards necessary to run his calculations through an IBM mainframe computer. He started to publish a newsletter called *American Investors Services* in 1956 that showed the relative strength rankings of the 1,000 stocks and 90 separate industry groups. At its height, Chestnutt's newsletter had roughly 100,000 subscribers paying an annual subscription of $250 for annual newsletter revenues of $25 million.

Hebert viewed Chestnutt as an important thought leader. In the early 1960s, the airline industry was being transformed economically by the conversion from propeller planes to jets. Institutional money managers had no interest in the sector and were predominantly focused on owning the overowned blue chip stocks. Chestnutt, based on his relative strength work, placed 25 percent of the fund in the airline group from the early 1960s through 1968. Additionally, he had a huge position in Xerox, which was the Apple of the 1960s. The fund's performance during this time left little doubt about the power of relative strength stocks in bullish markets.

The strongest stocks generally continue to be the strongest stocks. Winning streaks are persistent and predictable. Losing stocks generally continued to underperform. Chestnutt's stock management system was based on selecting the best-performing stocks from the best-performing industries. He paid almost no attention to Wall Street research. In a 1980 *Institutional Investor* article, Chestnutt described Wall Street research as follows: "It's garbage input and garbage output." Wall Street analysts are masters of writing a 100-page stock report without letting investors know whether they should buy or sell the stock. By following a relative strength price strategy, Chestnutt had created a winning discipline that served his investors with outperformance for three decades.

Chestnutt taught Mike how to chart the market. Although Chestnutt would laugh when Mike would try to sell him Hebert's relative strength statistics because he had his own, Chestnutt was willing to spend a lot of time with Mike teaching him the nuances of technical analysis and relative strength. Their friendship forged on the golf course warranted this.

Chestnutt's success attracted followers. William O'Neil, founder of the *Investor's Business Daily* (IBD) newspaper, is a believer and innovator in the area of relative strength. O'Neil invented a relative strength strategy that propelled him to become the top-performing broker in his firm in the early 1960s. At age 30, he was the youngest person at the time to buy a seat on the New York Stock Exchange, and he founded the William O'Neil + Co., Inc., brokerage firm in 1963. His firm is credited with being one of the first to create a computerized daily securities database in 1964. Today, IBD provides investors with computerized relative strength data on virtually every stock in the market.

The first hedge fund was founded by Alfred Winslow Jones in 1949. A. W. Jones had been a journalist for *Fortune* magazine doing an investigative report on technical methods of market analysis when he had the idea that he could buy the best stocks and short the worst stocks in a market-neutral manner to cancel out market risk and capture the performance of owning the best stocks and shorting the weakest stocks. With the right model, Jones also realized he could increase returns through the use of leverage. He was a loyal subscriber to Chestnutt's *American Investors Services* newsletter. In 1966, an article titled "The Jones Nobody Keeps Up With" by Carol Loomis showed that Jones's 10-year record was 87 percent better than that of the top-performing Dreyfus Fund. Over the next several years, more than 100 hedge funds were started.

As Mike reviewed his clients' portfolios in the early 1970s, it became clear that they were essentially creating random results with their stock picks. All the intelligence and efforts of equity managers at firms such as Pittsburgh National Bank, Chemical Bank, Bank of New York, and Manufacturers Hanover could be matched by throwing darts at the stock pages of the *Wall Street Journal* and investing in the stocks the darts hit. It was evident that relative to how the industry was doing, Mike, Chestnutt, Hebert, and O'Neil were on to something powerful with their relative strength discipline.

Mike was now in his late twenties. The first third of his life was drawing to a close. He had learned relative strength and technical analysis from some of the founding fathers of those investment practices. Although he understood and liked the idea of using a moving average crossover model to evaluate the attractiveness of the overall market and relative strength to evaluate individual stocks, Mike was comfortable with the belief that stocks generally appreciate over time and that one can make money in the markets without a lot of discipline as an investor by employing a buy-and-hold strategy. His sense of complacency was about to be shattered, and he would relearn the lessons of discipline, relative strength, and MAC the hard way.

Mike came to Wall Street as a sure way to get rich. His first two stocks had been huge winners. His father preached stocks. Why wouldn't he? His entire investable lifetime had run in parallel with good times in the stock market. All around Mike were Wall Street brokers making ridiculous money trading and owning stocks. In 1972, Mike made $82,000. For the son of a truck driver from Pittsburgh, that was a big deal. It was 10 times the annual income of the average American household. He had become convinced that the stock market was benign and stocks always went up.

Mike was fully engulfed in the whirlwind of a bullish stock market. Being a master of the universe on Wall Street can often give a person a sense of indestructibility. Mike knew he couldn't lose. He felt no fear when using an 18 percent margin to leverage into nonliquid assets. It was starting to get out of control.

From 1973 through 1974, the stocks in Mike's universe plummeted on average by 66 percent. Mike's personal fortunes suffered an almost immediate and complete reversal. What was considered a never-could-happen event happened. In the 1960s and early 1970s, the mantra was to own the "nifty fifty." The crowd herded into these 50 large cap stocks until they were extremely overbought. They were considered one-decision stocks. All you had to decide was to buy. Because of their steady appreciation, deciding when to buy was not important as investors expected the stocks to show steady appreciation for the indefinite future. Investors thought there would be no need to ever sell as these stocks had been extremely stable over a long period. In fact, Mike at the time felt it was dishonest to tell a person to buy a stock and later tell that person to sell it.

In two short years, the world changed. Mike went from being rich to being $180,000 in debt and essentially bankrupt.

By the end of 1974, Mike was a mess and out of a job. He had been floored by massive losses and was still in a state of shock from the devastation caused by the rapid downward move in the market. Because of his blind faith in stocks, he had failed to follow his own advice and sell all his stocks when the moving average crossover model signaled bearish conditions in advance of the market collapse. He was struggling to find something to grab on to so that he could begin the process of rebuilding his life. In a meeting with Merrill Lynch, Mike was pouring his heart out to a potential new employer. The Merrill guy's advice was to walk to the end office in his building, pour gasoline on himself, light himself on fire, and jump out the window. He pointed out that if Mike did that, at least he would be remembered for something.

In 1975, Mike caught a break when Smith Barney in San Francisco decided to hire him sight unseen. Smith Barney was a white-shoe, Princeton graduate–dominated firm. The Princeton boys had saturated their corner of the market and needed new talent to grow the firm. They needed more down and dirty producers who could grind for new business in places with which Princeton boys were unfamiliar. Mike had always been a top grinder and a leading producer. He moved west.

As Mike looked back into the smoking crater that marked the end of the first third of his life, he realized that one of his customers had been paying attention to the market timing and relative strength research Mike had been selling. It was Mr. Johnson, head portfolio manager at a large hedge fund. Johnson looked like the Hathaway shirt man as he was a distinguished, handsome man who wore a black patch over one eye. In just a few short years and with just one eye, Johnson could clearly see the value of staying out of major down markets. In 1973 and 1974, when the market tanked, Johnson's U.S. equity fund performed well by following the moving average crossover model to determine when the market was bullish or bearish and modifying its equity allocation accordingly. Johnson sidestepped the devastation in the equity market. Mike never forgot this lesson.

With the pain of 1973–1974 burned into his DNA, Mike never took his eye off the MAC market timing and relative strength signals he had learned in the early 1970s. Over almost 25 years, it was remarkable to Mike how consistently accurate those signals proved to be in a wide array of market conditions. In 1996, Mike began to manage money for investors willing to listen and trust his promise of staying out of major down markets.

Safety first to Mike was not about moderation or taking partial measures. At the start of 2000, he could not have told you in advance that the Nasdaq was about to drop by over 80 percent from high to low over the next several years. All he could be sure of was that he would sell his stock holdings without exception the instant his MAC market timing system said to get out. Mike avoided virtually all the major downturns in stocks during the 2000–2010 period, including the 55 percent high to low depreciation of the equity market during the credit crisis, by using his MAC model.

Mike spent a lifetime learning how to use a nonemotional, systematic method of knowing when the risk-reward balance of owning stocks was attractive and not attractive. Stock market bullish and bearish streaks are predictable and investable. They last long enough to offer an investor plenty of time to take advantage of the trend. Over the last 40 years, bullish intermediate-term trends have lasted an average of 22 weeks, and bearish intermediate-term trends about 14 weeks. Mike found a simple moving average crossover model that has reliably forecast winning and losing market trends from the early 1970s through today.

When the market is bullish, Mike buys high relative strength stocks. Strong stocks tend to stay strong. Winning streaks in stocks persist. Conversely, when the market is bearish, you don't want to own any stocks. Underperforming stocks tend to underperform with momentum to the downside. Losing streaks both in stocks and in the overall market tend to persist.

To learn and internalize the lesson of investable market streaks and the power of protecting wealth by getting out of the market during bearish periods, Mike had to get past the stock sermons of his father and tune out the nearly unanimous buy-and-hold doctrine. It took the first two-thirds of Mike's life for the lessons to be learned and for him to gain the faith necessary to take action on the basis of his discipline.

Mike's Takeaways

Mike's money management career was developing in a parallel time frame with the evolution of the buy-and-hold academic work of Sharpe, Samuelson, Jenson, Fama, and others. Because the buy-and-hold academic work had not completely overwhelmed the investment world in the 1960s and 1970s, Mike was able to view the trading landscape from a "what is" versus a "what should be" perspective. Mike's viewpoint is characterized by the following elements:

- Losses can be devastating and can take years to recover from. The most important risk in investing in stocks is the risk of significant loss in a major bear market. A fundamental element of risk management involves avoiding major losses. If losses are sufficiently large, it becomes increasingly likely that you will run out of time before you make back what has been lost.

- Avoiding major down markets is all about identifying bullish and bearish markets. When you identify a bearish market, get completely out. Mike never saw anyone make a lot of money in a bearish period or lose a lot of money in a bullish period. This is a statement about risk management. Bearish periods have asymmetric downside risk, whereas bullish markets have asymmetric upside opportunity.

- Like Sonny, Mike had to keep his emotions out of his trading behavior. He relied on quantitative systems that he started working with in the early 1970s to identify bullish and bearish intermediate-term market trends. Over the last 40 years, emotions have been an unreliable trade indicator whereas Mike's disciplined, automatic system has held up well in virtually all market conditions. Even when it felt uncomfortable, Mike stayed true to his discipline. By receiving his most important degree from the school of hard knocks, Mike learned this lesson thoroughly.

- When you are in a bullish period, invest aggressively. In Mike's case, he uses a well-diversified portfolio of high relative strength stocks. When one looks at the results of high relative strength stocks versus the overall market over most multiyear periods in modern market history, high relative strength stocks show measurable outperformance.

- Mike created a powerful combination of downside protection and upside participation. In major down markets, Mike is completely out of the stock market and in cash. In up markets, he owns the highest relative strength stocks. This combination offers investors strong up market capture with robust stop-loss characteristics on the downside.

CHAPTER EIGHT

Style

a. Technical, Fundamental, and Quants

Investors today generally approach the market from three different philosophical standpoints. The first group falls into the technical analysis and trend-following category. The second group can be classified as fundamental investors who consider company fundamentals (bottom-up analysis) and macroeconomic conditions (top-down analysis). The third group is composed of quants. *Quant* stands for "quantitative analysis" and has been described in the literature as financial econophysics and computational intelligence. This third group is usually found in the realm of alternative investing and mostly operates in hedge funds.

Technical, fundamental, and computational investing disciplines all live in a financial world that is given a theoretical structure by academic economists. Trading debt, currencies, futures, commodities, precious metals, derivatives, equities, and so on, is conducted every day at an incredible pace. With tremendous amounts of money and activity flowing, economists are always looking for ways to better explain what is going on. If they are able to create theories that make some sense of this activity and explain its inner workings, the hope is that the theory will produce guidelines for smart as opposed to lucky investing. The fact that economists try hard does not mean they are successful at understanding and explaining what is actually happening versus what appears to be happening. The global financial markets are incredibly complex. Securities trading is unlikely to be wrapped up by a simple academic model anytime in the near future.

Traders have an ear out for what is being said in the academic world. However, when the bell rings every morning at the market open, it is once again time to work with every available resource to make a living and deliver outperformance. When it is on the line in real time, traders fall back on what they believe in most. As the market transitions through various cycles, different strategies and theories will fit the market conditions best. Everything traders do can be judged instantaneously with hard numbers. There is no hiding. Although fundamental economic forces such as demand and supply are always at work, traders go well beyond academic theory in finding ways to gain an edge.

In 1884, Charles Dow and Edward Jones began to publish their Dow Jones stock market average consisting of nine railroad and two industrial stocks in a two-page newsletter called the *Customers' Afternoon Letter*. By 1896, the newsletter had 1,000 subscribers and they converted the letter into what is now called the *Wall Street Journal*. Charles Dow and statistician Edward Jones were two of the better known early technical analysis and trend-following investors.

Dow developed the Dow theory, which held that there is a strong, predictable relationship between stock market trends and general economic activity. When both Dow's industrial average and the railroad average (the transportation group of the time) moved in the same direction, it signaled that an important economic shift was occurring that would have some persistence. When both averages reached new highs, it signaled that a bull market was under way. Many investors continue to follow the Dow theory today.

Dow was followed by other technicians, such as Ralph Nelson Elliott, who discovered that market prices trend and reverse in predictable patterns. Elliott developed his theories and published his results in *The Wave Principle* in 1938. The Elliott Wave Principle continues to attract significant amounts of investor attention.

In essence, technical trading is founded on the efficient market theory, which states that stock prices contain all the information known by market participants. If stock prices are rising in an efficient market, it is likely that investors' perceptions about the future are improving. A rising stock or stock market is an indication of improving expected returns and/or a declining risk premium. A falling stock or stock market is an indication of deteriorating expected returns and/or a rising risk premium. The market is the single best indicator of market conditions. Where the academics and the traders differ is that technical traders believe prices will trend and academics argue that future prices fit a random distribution.

Some of the best known fundamental traders are Warren Buffett, Benjamin Graham, and Peter Lynch. Fundamental investors study companies and look for cases in which they believe the market does not fully appreciate the earnings power and/or asset value of a company. Like technical and quantitative analysts, they are actively selecting companies to invest in as they believe markets are not fully efficient and future stock prices can be predicted reliably enough to outperform the market portfolio.

Graham wrote that the market often exhibits irrational behavior. He believed that investors should be able to identify times when stocks are overvalued or undervalued by means of fundamental analysis. The primary assumption of Graham's approach is that stock prices ultimately have a fair or rational price in relation to future expected earnings and market participants will eventually move stocks to their fair/rational price levels.

Graham stated in his book *The Intelligent Investor*, "Investment is most intelligent when it is most businesslike." Warren Buffett regarded this comment as the most important words about investment ever written. What these words mean is that investing should be approached as a systematic, nonemotional process. Whether it is fundamental, technical, or quantitative, this is how investing is generally done in the institutional trading world.

Quantitative finance could not really get going until computers were widely available beginning in the 1980s. The purpose of applying heavy-duty computational power to market trading is to exploit for profit all the areas where economic theory and reality do not match up. In 2000, Rosario N. Mantegna and H. Eugene Stanley wrote *An Introduction to Econophysics*. They started their discussion with a reaction to efficient market hypothesis as follows:

> This is a strong, elegant and fruitful hypothesis, marred only by being quite wrong. Traders are not perfectly rational, and could not be. Markets are inefficient, both in microscopic ways (e.g., transaction costs), and in global ones, as shown by persistent "anomalies." Even over very short times, log price changes are non-Gaussian—the peaks are too sharp, while the tails are "fat," decaying too slowly, roughly as a power law. Worst of all, financial time series *are* predictable; though correlations in the price changes themselves quickly decay, nonlinear functions of price changes stay correlated over very long times. If markets are efficient, then prices are totally unpredictable; but prices are predictable; therefore markets are not efficient.

Institutional traders have been making a good living actively trading stocks for years. Although traders can argue that markets are highly efficient, partly efficient, or not efficient, institutional quants, technicians, and fundamental investors all agree that active management has value because stock prices are somewhat predictable.

Most experienced traders pay attention to as many factors as they can in an effort to tilt the odds in their favor. Whether they are technical, fundamental, or quant, they believe in active portfolio management. Through experience, they find the factors that are most closely associated with future stock price movement. In this book, we boil much of this institutional knowledge down to a usable strategy of staying out of major down markets and participating in major up markets.

The retail investment world, by contrast, is generally advised to buy and hold. For retail investors, the risk management tools provided boil down to asset allocation and diversification. In secular bear markets such as the ones from 1965 to 1982 and 2000 to 2012, absolute returns have been poor and portfolio volatility has been high. In light of the way the stock market traded from 2000 to 2012 and during other long secular bear periods (e.g., 1965 to 1982), active management warrants serious consideration.

b. Stocks, Bonds, and Options

In addition to the style of trading, most institutional investors are specialists in stocks, bonds, or options. Stock, bond, and options guys do not talk with one another much and approach the markets with very different perspectives. Bond guys are focused on balance sheet ratios and tend to look deeply into company fundamentals. Although most professional stock analysts and portfolio managers study income statements and balance sheets, many are persuaded into ownership by a company's product/service story. Options guys pay little attention to the company story and trade esoteric numbers called delta, gamma, and so on. Stock guys often say that bond guys are the smartest guys in the market. Bond guys, while knowing the numbers, tend to be high-momentum traders. Few people understand the options guys and have any clue about what they are doing.

We started our professional investment careers at Montgomery Securities selling growth stock research to growth mutual and hedge fund managers. Stock guys love a good story, and if you can supply a few numbers to bolster the case, all the better. When we moved to Susquehanna, the largest options market making firm in the world, and called our old equity fund manager contacts with "options market intelligence," we might as well have been speaking in Chinese. Their interest and willingness to use information from the options pits to trade their fundamental stories was practically nil. The only thing the equity guys really cared about was our annual poker tournament.

Susquehanna was founded by five ex-professional poker players. All employees were required to play poker daily. We had a full-sized Las Vegas poker table with plenty of cup holders installed next to our trading desks on the thirty-second floor of the glass tower at 101 California Street, San Francisco. Well-played poker is all about

making decisions with limited information on the basis of probabilities. This skill set translated well into options market making
and probabilities based investing. Once a year, we would host an
action-packed, prize-laden tournament for all our clients. Options
guys playing poker with equity guys was always good fun.

Jeff Yass, a founding member of Susquehanna and a subject in
the book *The New Market Wizards*, believes there are very close simi-
larities between playing poker and trading: "The basic concept that
applies to both poker and options trading is that the primary object
is not winning the most hands, but rather maximizing your gains."
Lots of investors are wrongly focused on their winning percentage,
in other words, the frequency with which an investment has a positive return rather than a negative return. What is far more important
than the frequency of wins versus losses is the magnitude of the wins
and losses.

As we moved into our own money management operations, we
worked closely with credit default swap (CDS), bond, and bond
derivatives traders. They had one of the best views into the workings
of the 2007–2009 credit crisis, as the crisis started with difficulties in
the bond market. While the equity world was dazed and confused,
many of the bond guys were often early and right. As long as credit
conditions were going into a deep freeze, it was easy to predict tough
times for equities. In 2009, as the credit market was being sorted out
and started to function again, some debt guys made the early call
for a new multiyear bull run for equities. Looking back, they clearly
called the bull equity market correctly in advance.

Bond bull markets often start because bond yields are attractive
relative to expected returns in other asset classes. At the equity bottom in 2009, the 10-year Treasury offered about a 5 percent return
and corporate junk debt (S&P rating of BB and below) offered yields
ranging from the low teens up into the 20 percent range. Partly out
of fear of owning equities and partly because of attractive yields,
money flows into the bond market. As the bond bull market matures,
yields fall and investors gradually move farther out on the risk curve
to obtain an attractive nominal yield. The pressure on institutional

bond buyers to keep buying bonds after the returns drop below what would be considered economically rational are enormous. A significant number of pension funds, insurance companies, and other traditional bond buyers are underperforming and desperate for higher returns because their return expectations are unrealistically high. New money keeps pouring into the bond market and needs to be put to work. At the end of 2012, the 10-year Treasury rate fell below 2 percent and junk debt was paying about 6.2 percent, an all-time low. Eventually, risk in the bond market is not adequately priced and the bond market experiences a negative imbalance between the default rate relative to yield. When this happens, there is significant risk for the equity market (as we saw in 2007–2009). The fear is that when the next credit crisis hits, governments will be so extended with debt from the last crisis that there will be no reserve to take aggressive corrective action.

It is this type of concern that should make every equity investor put in place a plan today for staying out of major down markets.

CHAPTER NINE

Your Brain on Stocks

THERE IS an entire field of finance based on human behavior biases called behavioral finance. The concept is founded on the idea that human beings greatly simplify the world around them and apply rules of thumb called heuristics to make decisions quickly. Some of these heuristics, in the view of behavioral finance, make people's trading behavior somewhat predictable. Human bias can lead to seemingly irrational behavior that is a violation of the underlying financial theory assumption that profit-seeking, rational people create efficient markets.

Our minds do a very good job of seeing causality in a linear form. Most people do not intuitively assign probabilities and evaluate probabilistic outcomes well. Studies of human decision making conclude that if we conducted a careful analysis of all the decisions we are faced with during a day, we would be bogged down by analysis and virtually unable to get out of bed. Optimization of every single choice we face, including putting one foot in front of the other, would overwhelm any known supercomputer. Rather than performing detailed analysis on everything we do, we often make decisions by using our emotions rather than pure analytics.

Neurobiologists believe that human brains have three levels. The first and most primitive level is the reptilian brain, which manages many core functions such as breathing and heartbeat. The second level of brain computational activity occurs in the limbic brain, which manages our emotions. This portion of the brain is shared by all mammals. The third level of brain function is the cognitive brain, where high-level thought and analytics are computed.

Patients who have undergone brain surgery that involves destroying or removing the limbic (emotional) brain area struggle to make decisions even at the most basic level. Decisions are carefully considered, but no final decision can be reached. The point of all of this is that much trading activity is based on human emotions.

This partly explains why investors will ride a position all the way down only to give up at the bottom. Their emotions are going crazy as they experience increasing amounts of loss until finally it is unbearable. The exact time when they reach the point of maximum emotional pain is about where markets often find their lows. Figure 9.1 shows a graph of market sentiment as measured by the American Association of Individual Investors (AAII). As you can see, in March 2009 and September 2010, sentiment tends to bottom at market bottoms. Extreme bearish market sentiment measured on a historical basis is often used as an indication of an oversold market that is about to rally.

Because a large proportion of risk perceptions come from an emotional part of the brain, investors are prone to overreact in either direction. Feelings of fear or complacency can be carried too far. These emotions can often change dramatically in a matter of hours or minutes on the basis of a news flash or another extraneous input. An emotions-based view of market trading goes a long way toward

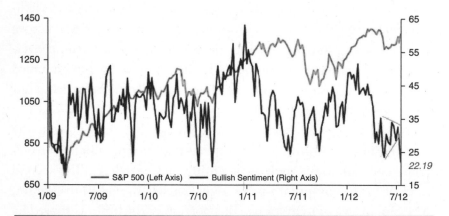

FIGURE 9.1 Investor Sentiment Tends to Bottom at Market Lows

Source: AAII and Bespoke Investment Group.

explaining why Yale economist Robert Shiller found that stock prices move much more than changes in earnings would suggest.

Because risk perceptions are tied to emotion, they usually change far more rapidly and dramatically than do explicit earnings expectations. Calculating forward earnings is a cognitive exercise that usually requires a spreadsheet and analytic reasoning. It is generally not considered an emotional experience. When investors are scared and in a panic sell mode, they usually throw out formal earnings projections as being not relevant. Their emotions are telling them that expected earnings are headed lower.

Part of the argument against market timing is based on the idea that investors in the aggregate make really bad market timing decisions. This argument is generally correct. Figure 9.2 shows how money tends to flow into the stock market near peaks and out at troughs.

According to a research report from J.P. Morgan, the average investor has achieved an average annualized return of 2.6 percent over the 20-year period 1991–2010 versus a 7.7 percent return for the S&P 500 and an inflation rate of 2.4 percent. Figure 9.3 reinforces the idea that individual investors in the aggregate tend to raise cash at market lows and overinvest in stocks at market peaks.

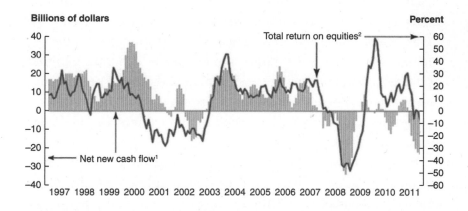

FIGURE 9.2 Funds Flow into Stocks Near Market Highs and Out Near Market Lows

[1]Net new cash flow to equity funds is plotted as a six-month moving average.
[2]The total return on equities is measured as the year-over-year change in the MSCI All Country World Daily Total Return Index.

Source: Inventory Company Institute and Morgan Stanley Capital International.

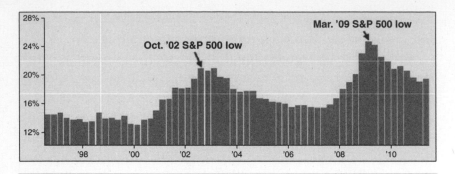

FIGURE 9.3 Cash as a Percentage of Total Household Financial Assets
Source: Morgan Stanley Capital International.

Morningstar, the market data firm that ranks mutual funds, has detected a widespread pattern of investors chasing past results by pouring money in after a fund has done well and taking it out after the fund falters. Investors who favor managed funds can be more susceptible to making poor timing decisions because a fund will often perform well after a period of underperformance and perform poorly after a period of outperformance.

It is highly likely that individual investors are not using a disciplined, systematic trading system to make their market timing decisions. It is likely that they are basing decisions on both emotion and real-life financing needs. Stock market lows are often associated with times of high unemployment and housing market downturns. In 2007, the U.S. unemployment rate was running in the mid-4 percent range. In mid-2009, the unemployment rate was running in the mid-9 percent range and remained above 8 percent for the next three years.

Figure 9.4 shows what happened to home prices during the last recession in 2008 and 2009.

It is quite possible that investors pull money out of stocks at market bottoms not only because they are struggling with their emotional decision making but also because they need the money as they have lost their jobs, their liquid assets are worth less, and they may be underwater on their home mortgages. In times of financial stress, people pull money from wherever they have liquidity. Selling stocks is a source of liquidity.

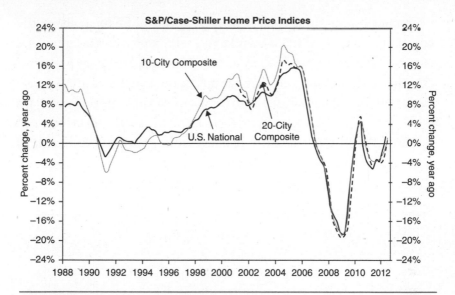

FIGURE 9.4 The Home Price Collapse in the Great Recession

Source: S&P, Dow Jones Indices, and Fiserv.

Conversely, during market peaks, unemployment rates are usually low and other asset classes are showing strong pricing trends. Investors during bullish times have excess capital to put to work. It is quite likely that much of the buying and selling of stock by individuals has more to do with their personal balance sheets and emotional reactions to current market conditions than with their executing on a well-considered market timing strategy.

In any event, the human experience tends to strongly suggest that nonsystematic, emotional market timing decisions are frequently made and result in underperformance relative to a buy-and-hold approach. This has caused some market observers to arrive at the conclusion that market timing does not work. The evidence that basing stock buy/sell decisions on emotions is usually a suboptimal strategy is strong.

This evidence has masked the success of market timing decisions made by quantitative, disciplined nonemotional trading systems. In sharp contrast to emotion-based trading, there is a long history of success of market timing based on systematic approaches, including using a simple moving average crossover model.

From a successful market timing perspective, understanding the emotional content of stock buying and selling provides a significant clue to when to buy and when to sell. Fear and greed are powerful emotions. These emotions drive a significant amount of stock accumulation and distribution, and they can cause a market to trend downward if collective fear is rising or trend higher if collective greed is rising. They directly relate to people's willingness to take on risk. If we determine the direction of risk perceptions, we have a very good chance of predicting stock prices in the aggregate over the near term and intermediate term.

CHAPTER TEN

Observations from the Trading Floor of an Investment Bank

W E HAVE had a front-row seat in the money management business at the institutional level for years. In Chapter 9, we talked about poor investment decisions caused by the influence of human emotions. In this chapter, we talk about distortions in the institutional trading market from the perspective of a sell-side investment bank. What is evident from our experience is that there are times when market pricing could hardly be called rational and efficient. More important, knowing how institutions behave offers investors more insight into how and when to trade stocks.

In the dark hours of the early morning on the largest trading floor west of Manhattan before the market open in the middle and late 1990s, head trader Bobby would yell, "I love the smell of napalm in the morning." This was a line spoken by the character Kilgore (played by Robert Duvall) in the movie *Apocalypse Now*. Kilgore then goes on to say that it smells like victory. With trillions of dollars flowing through an industry filled with macho, adrenaline-fueled trading junkies excited by the possibility of outsized bonuses, market pricing can become distorted in a predictable way.

In Chapter 6 we discussed the theory of efficient markets. The efficient market hypothesis is a cornerstone of the buy-and-hold approach to stock investment. Rather than argue the merits of the efficient market hypothesis on an academic level, we share with you our observations from having spent years on the trading desks of several major institutional sell-side firms. The purpose of these observations is to provide you with a deeper and richer understanding of the array of factors that influence stock prices. These observations demonstrate that stock prices are influenced by oddities in human behavior that often cause security pricing to be predictable.

a. The Sell-Side Analyst Conundrum and How Earnings Momentum Can Be Predictable

Rational people with high-paying jobs usually want to keep their jobs. If the job is to predict the future, analysts are far more likely to keep their jobs in the short run if they predict the average of what everyone else is predicting rather than stepping out on a limb and diverging from the consensus by a significant amount. If the prediction is in line with consensus expectations and the analysts are wrong, they are wrong along with everyone else. If the prediction is far from the mean and an analyst is wrong, he or she must be deficient since everyone else knew the answer.

Investment banks pay their senior analysts well. The job is prestigious, and analysts are considered experts. Analysts are eager to keep their jobs and as a result are usually hesitant to make predictions that stray from the conventional view. If they do have a differentiated viewpoint, it is often expressed only in verbal comments to their best clients rather than written in their formal research reports.

When a company reports meaningfully better than expected earnings and revenues, analysts will perform their checks with management and the broader industry. If a secular change is under way, analysts may adjust their forward estimates only modestly higher as they want to make sure a new trend is under way and would rather not diverge too far from the mean estimate. As several more earnings cycles pass, analysts frequently and with chronic persistence underestimate actual earnings. Over time, the sell-side investment analyst community becomes less relevant to the investment process as mutual fund and hedge fund money managers are willing to jump on board the better earnings reports faster than do sell-side equity analysts.

The cycle of exceeding analysts' estimates is often predictable in light of the pressures on analysts to be overly conservative. Stocks that consistently beat estimates often become momentum stocks that demonstrate considerably better performance than the average stock during their outperformance cycle. This dynamic helps explain why there is a large group of institutional stock buyers focused on momentum or high relative strength stocks.

Just as predictably as stocks rise on repeated better-than-expected earnings, they fall sharply when they miss the estimates. Often they miss consensus earnings estimates after a long winning streak more because the analysts become overly aggressive in raising estimates than because of a fundamental change in the company's operations.

While the company is beating earnings steadily, a conservative sell-side analyst becomes a less important part of the investment process for the institutional buy-side customer. To get back into the game, a sell-side analyst may jump out ahead of the pack with an aggressive forecast. If the forecast is right, this analyst is now the go-to guy on the stock and has regained his or her position as an important part of the institutional investment process.

Other analysts now follow with equally aggressive if not more aggressive estimates. As expectations ratchet well above what may be thought of as reasonable, the company is exposed to a high risk of missing the elevated expectations and the stock may experience a rapid pullback as momentum investors sell without concern for the underlying fundamentals. Institutional investors may sell the stock for days, weeks, and months. Some stocks eventually recover. Many never come back.

For those who tie their stock purchasing to the expected earnings power of a company, this series of events can explain how momentum investing is a somewhat predictable event. It describes how those who trade in information do not have a firm grasp of what the information is and are slow to release more accurate information into the market. It helps explain how the connection between the price/earnings ratio and the stock price can become disjointed on high relative strength stocks relative to the market P/E multiple. It also explains why so many momentum stocks eventually and predictably suffer a severe price decline.

We are not the only ones to observe that stock momentum driven by earnings is somewhat predictable and investable. There have been a number of academic studies on "post-earnings-announcement drift," including Ball and Brown (1968); Foster, Olsen, and Shevlin (1984); and Bernard and Thomas (1989), to name a few. The Foster, Olsen, and Shevlin study found that over the 60 trading days after an earnings announcement, a long position in stocks with unexpected earnings in the highest decile, combined with a short position in stocks in the lowest decile, yields an annualized "abnormal" return of about 25 percent before transaction costs. The stock drift over time based on publicly announced earnings suggests that traders are failing to assimilate available information (which is what appears to be happening with the sell-side analyst community) and/or that there is some failure of the capital asset pricing model (CAPM) to adjust for changing risk premiums.

b. Institutional Stock Buyers

The largest mutual funds control trillions of dollars of stock. They can hold large percentages of a company's stock that dwarf in relative size the average daily volume of that stock that is traded. In 1995, the Fidelity Magellan fund owned more than 5 percent of the market capitalization of 266 companies. In other words, if the fund bought or sold the stock aggressively, it probably would have a significant impact on the stock price.

There are investors who pay very close attention to what stocks the large mutual funds own. If a fund underowns a stock relative to its benchmark and the stock is showing strong relative strength, it is likely that the fund will increase its holdings. David O'Leary, president of Alpha Equity Research in Portsmouth, New Hampshire, specialized in tracking Fidelity's holdings. O'Leary discovered that when Fidelity owned less than 5 percent of a company's outstanding shares and then boosted its ownership to 12 percent, the stock would appreciate by 55 percent on average (see "The Thorn in Fidelity's Side," *U.S. News & World Report*, September 8, 1997, pp. 72–73). In 1995, it is estimated that Fidelity's trades made up between 5 and 7 percent of the total traded volume on the New York Stock Exchange.

If a large fund decides to liquidate a major position, it can take days and be devastating to the stock price. Overowned stocks carry this risk. Mutual funds report their holdings quarterly, and there are many Internet-based services that provide information about who the top owners of a stock are.

Smaller investors can actively take advantage of the larger funds' stock movements by getting ahead of their trades. Having many small funds buying and selling in addition to the large funds can make entry and exit prices worse for the big funds. Partly as a result of this trading problem, many of the larger funds became early adopters of dark pools and other trading systems that make it harder to see their trading activities.

One tactic occasionally used by large funds was to manipulate a stock price by withdrawing approval for the brokerage firm to lend its stock out to short sellers. To short sell a stock, securities law requires that investors borrow it before selling it short. Although there have been abuses of this requirement, many short sellers do secure what is termed a locate on stock before they short it. What this means is that brokerage firms such as Goldman Sachs and Morgan Stanley that hold stocks for the benefit of major institutional accounts lend the long stock for a price to short sellers with the prior approval of the stockholder.

Short sellers who receive notice that their borrowed stock is being recalled have to buy the stock in the open market and return it to their broker. If a stock recall is done in sufficient size, the long stock fund holder (typically a mutual fund) can cause a very powerful short squeeze in a stock by recalling all of its shares "on borrow."

A short squeeze occurs when short sellers rush to buy stock back as the security is showing strong appreciation and their losses are mounting. Because the buying pressure is far larger than the normal supply from ordinary selling, prices can be bid up dramatically. A dramatic example of a short squeeze was when the federal government placed a ban on short selling financial stocks in the United States in 2008. Some heavily shorted securities jumped by over 100 percent in a single day as short sellers scrambled to cover.

Large stockholders looking to exit a position may induce a short squeeze as a way to create buying interest in the stock they are selling. By calling in the stock loans, they create heavy, nonregular buying pressure. It is hard to call this price action random. In evaluating whether to buy or sell a stock, it is important to take note of the major holders of the security.

c. Cross-Asset Class Price Manipulation

Large hedge funds can move markets and often do. Large hedge funds today manage billions of dollars in a single fund. They can trade in almost any type of security (stocks, bonds, commodities, options, credit default swaps, futures contracts, etc.). They have no qualms about moving money fast. We know from personal experience that hedge funds can have 100 percent turnover in a single day, and 100 percent or greater daily turnover is not uncommon.

As a result of the movement of so much money so fast, buy-sell imbalances can be created and exploited. For example, the options market is a zero-sum game. When an investor buys a call, a market maker sells a call to facilitate the transaction. With the market maker short the call, he or she is exposed to the stock appreciating and getting called. To hedge away this risk, market makers often buy stock when they are short calls. Options market makers generally trade on what is called a delta-neutral basis. If a hedge fund buys calls aggressively from several market makers on a single stock, the stock is likely to trade higher as the market makers put on their long stock hedge. If the hedge fund was long the stock before buying the calls and was interested in selling the stock, its options buying might create a natural buyer for its stock position.

This type of cross-asset class price manipulation can be conducted in a variety of markets and a variety of ways. Many of the successful high-frequency trading hedge funds today are masters of this game. In this case, funds are essentially using their buying or selling power to distort market prices over the short run to favor their trades. This can hardly be called a random or efficient process, and individual investors should be hesitant to read too much into short-term price fluctuations.

d. Information Distortions

Portfolio managers have been known to publicly talk up a stock while they are selling. We have seen portfolio managers attend crowded institutional conferences and ask company management questions designed to give a favorable impression of the stock and the portfolio manager's attitude toward that stock. Other investors take note and help create buying pressure while the initial manager is selling. The practice of talking up or down a stock can occur in conferences, in newspapers, and on TV. Be careful about reacting too quickly to everything you read or hear.

Big money management is a highly competitive industry. Successful managers make millions. With the stakes high, managers are under tremendous pressure to gain an advantage. What is said about the markets or about individual securities by institutional investors should be taken with a grain of salt and be just one piece of your investment process mosaic.

e. Investment Period End Markups and Markdowns

At the end of a quarter, institutional investors often rebalance their portfolios by buying winning stocks and selling losers. Part of what drives this behavior is the requirement that many institutions report their holdings to investors at the end of a reporting period.

Winning stocks often trade higher and weak stocks often trade lower at quarter end.

There is an even more active markup that can occur in certain less liquid stocks. As the trading day is expiring on the last day of a quarter, institutions may flood the market with buy orders to rapidly mark the price of the targeted stocks higher. Although the price may immediately adjust back down to where it was before the markup on the open of the next trading day, the fund's performance is measured through the close of the prior day.

Depending on the fund and the power of the markup, fund performance can be materially enhanced. It is possible to anticipate what stocks may be marked up. Look at the list of highly institutionally owned emerging growth company stocks, which are often strong candidates for a good markup.

f. Unequal Information Distribution

Big institutional buy-side clients (hedge and mutual funds) pay millions of dollars in commissions to sell-side brokerage firms. Because of the amount of money being paid, sell-side firms strive to make their buy-side clients happy. Sell-side firms often distinguish themselves with their largest clients by providing insightful investment ideas early.

When making outbound calls or scheduling customer visits, sell-side research analysts generally call their largest accounts first. Analysts who can stimulate trading activity on their firm's desk in their coverage list (the group of stocks that the analyst publishes research on) are often the highest paid. Influential and top-tier sell-side analysts are occasionally hired away by a buy-side client willing to offer even higher pay.

Institutional brokerage phone lines generally are not recorded. This is true even on the trading floors. Thus, although the written word (research report) is scrutinized to make sure it complies with all industry laws and regulations, the phone lines remain in the "Wild West" of trading. Institutional sell-side salespeople can often tell from an analyst's body language that a rating change is coming. The sales force will advise its clients to be in position in case a rating change does come. Analysts themselves may provide clues directly to their best accounts that change is in the air.

This provides some explanation of why trading earnings reports can be so difficult. With an earnings report, investors have to predict two important outcomes. The first is whether the company will meet, beat, or miss earnings expectations. The second is how the stock will react to the news. It is often the case that a stock will trade up on a miss and down on a beat. This occurs because so much money was positioned for the event in advance of the news and it moves counter to the direction of the event as a way to take profits when the news is announced.

As Nicholas Maier pointed out in his memoir about working with Cramer & Company, "If you believe the everyday investor gets the same level of service (and trading advantage) as someone like Jim Cramer (Cramer & Company, a high commission paying institutional firm), you probably should stop trading now."

Because the playing field is not entirely level, it is difficult to consistently make money as a retail investor trading on known catalysts such as earnings reports or U.S. Food and Drug Administration announcements. To somewhat level the playing field, retail investors should focus more on catching trends than on day-trading news flow.

g. The Institutional Stock Marketing Process

Institutional stock marketing is not that different from the marketing of many other products. Investment banks battle to win IPO underwriting fees partly on the basis of their ability to market (sponsor) a stock. They convince company management teams that their investment bank has the best analysts and the most loyal institutional investor following. Once a company has gone public, sell-side investment banks take the company on road shows to tell its story to investors. They invite companies to speak at conferences. The analyst covering the stock is given more time to talk about the story with the sales team, and that influences the message coming from the bank about what stocks to buy. The more the stock is shown and the story is talked up, all else being equal, the higher the stock usually trades.

Occasionally, in advance of a corporate stock issuance, investment banks will issue glowing reports about a stock in an attempt to win favor with management teams. The stock trades higher. With the stock elevated, the company announces a follow-on offering that takes advantage of the higher price. It should not come as much of a surprise that the underwriters on the stock offering are often the same firms that published the bullish research reports. A ratings downgrade by a firm that does not win the underwriting business is not uncommon.

In a purely efficient market, it would not make sense that talking more about what is already known would have a predictable impact on stock price. If marketing works—that is, gives what is already public information more emphasis—it is hard to argue that the stock market and the pricing mechanism are perfectly efficient.

Some investors monitor the company marketing calendars of the major investment banks and the conference schedules of corporations as an input into their stock buying process. Buying a stock that is getting rising institutional support is a way to improve the odds of having a successful investing experience.

h. The Insider and Private Equity Information Advantage

Private equity firms are institutions that provide growth capital to emerging companies before the companies offer their stock to the public on a listed exchange. Their expertise lies in identifying winning products, services, and management teams and nurturing them with money, expertise, and networking until they have attained the critical mass to be suitable for an initial public offering or acquisition by another company. These investment firms tend to have very deep industry domain knowledge and an understanding of what is happening on the frontier of the investment space.

Whereas sell-side investment banks and their largest clients can have better information than many other investors, private equity investors and company managements can have even better information. Investment banks are experts in financial markets but may not have the same depth of industry knowledge as private equity firms and senior members of company management teams.

An example of this was the initial public offering (IPO) of Zynga (ZNGA) on December 16, 2011, and its subsequent trading history during 2012. Zynga is a social game maker whose games are played on websites such as Facebook (FB). It was played up as San Francisco's fastest growing start-up and was a poster child for the hot trend of social media.

The IPO was priced at $10 per share, and eventually the stock traded up to a closing high of $14.69 in March 2012. In early April, Zynga's chief executive officer sold 15 percent of his stock holdings for roughly $198 million, or $12 per share. What was notable about this stock offering is that it came two months ahead of when the official insider selling lockup was scheduled to end.

At the end of July with the stock trading near $5 per share, Zynga missed second-quarter analyst earnings and revenue estimates and lowered its FY2012 earnings guidance to $0.04–$0.09 from $0.23–$0.29. Management indicated that the company's earnings were heavily back-end-loaded, with most of the earnings occurring in the second half of the year. The shock was magnified by the fact that the company had raised its guidance earlier in the year.

The stock immediately gapped lower by about 40 percent and has been trading near $2.50 per share through the time of this writing. The company is currently trading for less than the $2.7 billion worth of cash, receivables, and real estate shown on the balance sheet at the end of the second quarter.

The special follow-on offering allowing the CEO to unload shares well before the lockup expired sent a strong signal to hedge funds that it was a good bet to sell short ZNGA shares in size. Short sellers understood the CEO's information advantage and acted on it. Short interest measured by days to cover peaked in late February and remained elevated through May. It was clear to the institutional trading market following the smart insider money that ZNGA was going down.

In August, the CEO purchased a $16 million, seven-bedroom mansion in Pacific Heights, San Francisco. Meanwhile, the company's nonexecutive employees who were not given the right to sell before the original lockup date expiration and virtually all the public shareholders suffered significant losses. Many of the employees who were expecting to "make bank" on the IPO were then holders of worthless stock options and were looking for a better place to work. The chief operating officer was gone. Numerous shareholder lawsuits were filed. Competitor Electronic Arts (EA) launched a copyright infringement lawsuit accusing Zynga of copying EA's "Sims Social" with its "The Ville" game. The negative feedback loop was spooling up.

The pricing of the Facebook IPO is another case of uneven information flows. The FB IPO was one of the most hyped events in recent memory in Silicon Valley, with numerous articles talking about how much early FB investors had made and how powerful the company had become as the leading social media investment play. It did not hurt to have a full-length feature film, *The Social Network*, distributed about the company showing incredible growth and describing founder Mark Zuckerberg as a genius in advance of the IPO. The promotion of FB was effective in stimulating the blinding effects of greed.

Halfway through the Facebook IPO road show (when the company management meets with institutional investors before going public), the lead underwriters, Morgan Stanley (MS), JPMorgan (JPM), and Goldman Sachs (GS), reduced their earnings forecasts. According to Reuters, this came as a surprise to many institutional investors as it was released so close to the stock's public debut. The downward earnings revision was a result of management updating the prospectus to caution investors about the challenges of moving the FB application from the desktop to mobile applications. This material information was actively provided to big institutional clients, placing other investors at an information disadvantage. Investors outside this institutional information circle would have had to read the updated prospectus and make their own assumptions to discover the possibility of negative earnings revisions on their own.

On Friday, May 18, 574 million shares of Facebook traded in its first day of trading, which was 21.4 percent of the total volume of the Nasdaq Composite. The Facebook IPO was another classic case of insider selling. Of the 421 million shares offered, 241.2 million shares were from early investors with an average per share cost of about $1. Insiders walked away with approximately $9.2 billion on the deal. The company received about $6.8 billion. The IPO was priced at the high end of the range, which worked well for sellers and placed new buyers at a greater risk of loss. Within three months, retail investors who received stock on "the deal" were looking at a roughly 50 percent loss.

The story goes on. Reminiscent of the early stock sale made by the Zynga CEO, the first venture capitalist to invest in Facebook and a director of the company, Peter Thiel, announced in August 2012 that he sold roughly 20.1 million shares of stock for $395.8 million well before the November lockup expiration for employees. On the IPO, Thiel sold $640.1 million, bringing his Facebook net proceeds to roughly $1 billion. The 20.1 million shares sold in August represented the majority of Thiel's remaining holdings, leaving him with 5.6 million shares. By early September, the value of Facebook had declined by $50 billion.

The conclusion to draw from this story is that the market, through the actions of the most informed participants, will often give you powerful information. When informed market participants act in a public manner, it is often a good idea to take notice. Counter to what random and efficient markets are expected to do, it can take days, weeks, or months for the full ramifications of public information about the actions of in-the-know investors to be fully priced into stocks.

i. Trade What Is Versus What You Want It to Be

If you asked experienced traders why stocks go up and down, you might be told that there are more buyers than sellers or there are more sellers than buyers. This explanation seems to lack any meaningful fundamental information, but it is often used by the most experienced market practitioners. Stock movement may have nothing to do with economic or financial theory for periods of time. This is a really important point to remember.

Experienced institutional stock, bond, and options traders take most financial theory with a grain of salt—things happen. Stuff that falls outside of any textbook takes place in the securities markets regularly. This is why when you listen to or read the financial news at the end of the day explaining why the market went up or down, you should be highly skeptical. Securities trading and markets are a complex place that is not well defined by the social sciences or the news media.

The great economist Paul A. Samuelson of the Department of Economics at MIT served on the board of directors of a company called Addison-Wesley. When he resigned from the board, Samuelson decided that he wanted to sell all his shares in Addison-Wesley. The problem was that the stock was thinly traded on the pink sheets. Samuelson was certain that his selling of his shares would cause the stock to trade lower as a result of increased supply. In fact, all the thousands of readers of Samuelson's textbook *Economics* (1948, 1980; Samuelson and Nordhaus, 1985, 2010) would have known that an increase in stock supply should be expected to lower price.

What actually happened was that Samuelson's selling activity increased the trading flow and liquidity of the stock. As a result, brokers who had previously not known or cared about the stock started to take an interest. Motivated brokers generated increased buying interest in the stock, resulting in rising prices. Thus, although Samuelson's selling should have taken the stock lower according to his own writings, the real world proved to be more complex and less predictable. In the wake of this incident, Samuelson said, "When someone preaches 'Economics is one lesson,' I advise: Go back for the second lesson" (*Annual Review of Financial Economics,* 2009, 1:19–35).

It is important that you get comfortable with this concept. By being open-minded about why stocks move, you will not become too emotionally tied to a stock or the market. The world does not necessarily follow the script found in a textbook.

CHAPTER ELEVEN

Risk

TALKING ABOUT financial risk is like peeling back the layers of an onion. Risk is a multilayered, multifaceted beast by nature. Financial theory defines risk mostly as volatility. Risk to us is outliving your savings. Risk is having your money waste away relative to inflation. Risk is a knockdown in your investment portfolio that is so severe that the loss is effectively permanent. Risk to an equity investor is having one's investment life overlap with a period in stock market history when stocks do not advance.

Warren K. Greene, former president of American Investors Fund and the No Load Mutual Fund Association, points out that "you can spend a lifetime in the market and not see steady appreciation." Greene's prime career years stretched from 1966 to 1985. From the high in 1966 to the low of 1982, the DJIA declined by roughly 22 percent. By 1985, the DJIA had averaged less than 1 percent average annual appreciation per year. In the middle of Green's investment career, he endured the 1973–1974 market collapse. That downturn felt much worse to Greene than did the 2008–2009 drop. It was the final knockdown of a market that had been seeing narrowing leadership since 1968. Roughly 50 percent of brokers went out of business shortly after 1974.

The bear market that occurred from September 7, 1929, to July 8, 1932, saw the market fall 86.2 percent. The market did not recover to its previous highs until 1954. An investment of $10,000 in the Nasdaq at the 2000 peak was worth roughly $6,000 in mid-2012.

With the benefit of hindsight and an almost 200-year history of equity market trading, it is reasonable to conclude that markets always come back. The question is, Will they come back within your time frame? Historically, when the S&P 500 has declined by 20 percent or more, it has taken an average 6.5 years to reach its old highs.

As Malcolm Gladwell pointed out in his book *Outliers*, when you are born can have a far bigger effect on how your life works out than does your intelligence. We are all born market timers. The very act of being born is an act of market timing. So are going to college, getting married, buying a house, having kids, sending the kids to college, retiring, and dying. These events in our lives can often trigger the buying and selling of equities. This basic fact of nature on its own essentially invalidates the viability of a buy-and-hold market approach.

Most people do most of their investing over a 20-year period from their middle to late forties to their early to middle sixties. Depending on when you were born, you could have excellent or poor investment results based on how your prime investment years overlap with market supercycles. If you started your investment career in 2000 with an assumption that you would achieve an average annual nominal return of 8 percent over the next two decades, you now need to bump up your investment return rate to 21 percent to stay on track with your original objective. No wonder so many baby boomers have decided to stay in the work world longer.

If your primary investment years were the 1970s, you would have had a tough time growing wealth with a buy-and-hold strategy. Figure 11.1 shows $1 million in net worth held in bonds, housing, and stocks growing to only $1.1 million from 1966 through 1980.

In contrast, if the bulk of your personal investment cycle overlapped the 1981–2000 period, you probably did very well (Figure 11.2). In this example, $1 million grows to $4.2 million. How many of us thought we knew everything we needed to know about how to invest after the bull run of the 1980s and 1990s?

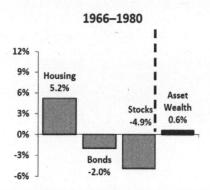

FIGURE 11.1 Asset Growth, 1966–1980

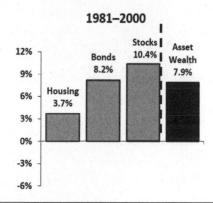

FIGURE 11.2 Asset Growth, 1981–2000

Source: Safehaven.com, April 5, 2011.

History shows that the stock market moves in what are called supercycles. Figure 11.3 depicts the appreciation of the Dow Jones Industrials (DJI) from 1896 through 2011. What is immediately evident is that the market is stair stepping higher with long periods of no net appreciation and high volatility (dark areas) separated by shorter periods of rising markets (light areas).

What the last 115 years of market history teaches us is that a choppy-sideways market (dark areas in the figure) is not uncommon and can persist for years. In fact, a large portion of the area (63 percent) in the chart is shaded dark. It is clear that experiencing long periods

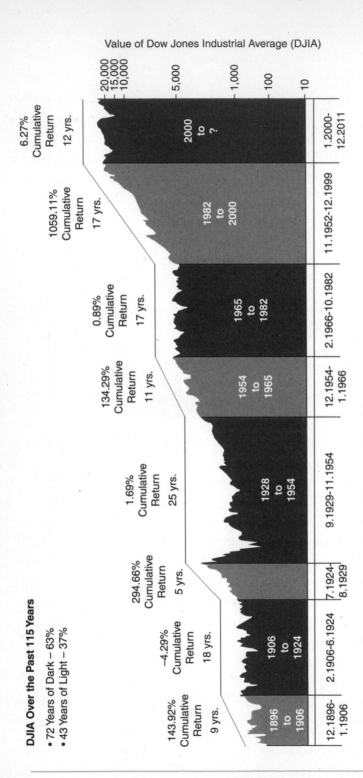

Value of Dow Jones Industrial Average (DJIA)

DJIA Over the Past 115 Years

• 72 Years of Dark – 63%
• 43 Years of Light – 37%

143.92%
Cumulative
Return
9 yrs.

-4.29%
Cumulative
Return
18 yrs.

294.66%
Cumulative
Return
5 yrs.

1.69%
Cumulative
Return
25 yrs.

134.29%
Cumulative
Return
11 yrs.

0.89%
Cumulative
Return
17 yrs.

1059.11%
Cumulative
Return
17 yrs.

6.27%
Cumulative
Return
12 yrs.

1896
to
1906

1906
to
1924

1928
to
1954

1954
to
1965

1965
to
1982

1982
to
2000

2000
to
?

| 12.1896-1.1906 | 2.1906-6.1924 | 7.1924-8.1929 | 9.1929-11.1954 | 12.1954-1.1966 | 2.1966-10.1982 | 11.1952-12.1999 | 1.2000-12.2011 |

Logarithmic graph of the Dow Jones Industrial Average from 12/1896 through 12/2011.
Source: Graph Created by Guggenheim Investments using data from www.dowjones.com 01/2012

Performance displayed represents past performance, which is no guarantee of future results. The Dow Jones Industrial Average is unmanaged and unavailable for direct investment. Returns do not reject any dividends, management fees, transaction costs or expenses. Contact your financial advisor to discuss the concept further.

FIGURE 11.3   **Dow Jones Industrial Average Price Chart, 1896–2011**

of underperformance in stocks is not an outlier event. The figure clearly illustrates the fallacy that if you wait about 20 years, your investments will work out just fine with a buy-and-hold model.

Market commentators and financial advisors often site long-term average annual market appreciation rates of roughly 7 percent. They then use this long-term average as the expected rate of return in your portfolio. What Figure 11.3 shows is that although the average rate of appreciation over 115 years is roughly 7 percent, it is either roughly 0 percent or 14 percent for long periods. Because personal investment periods tend to be roughly 20 to 40 years, it is unlikely that many of us will experience the 115-year average return.

During dark periods, the stock market is often subjected to panic sell-offs. Roughly 18 percent of the time over the last 20 years, the market has experienced a major downturn. Watching your portfolio lose 20 to 50 percent of its value periodically is unpleasant, and the situation is made worse by the fact that returns are asymmetric.

A 50 percent loss of principal requires 100 percent appreciation to get back to breakeven. Years of gains can be wiped out in a few short months of down market action. It usually takes much longer to build wealth than to lose it. This is why losses are so much more painful than gains are joyful. What matters in investing is not the frequency of your winning investments but the cumulative size of your losing investments relative to your winning investments (Figure 11.4).

To our knowledge, there is no reason to believe that a 100 percent return is more likely to occur immediately after a 50 percent loss. In other words, the act of losing money does not make getting it back any easier. Therefore, it seems worthwhile to not only attempt to capture market gains but also have some mechanism to at least attempt to minimize losses. By definition, this requires some sort of active management strategy.

One of the central arguments for staying invested in the market at all times is the concept that a large proportion of market advance comes during a short period that is nearly impossible to predict in

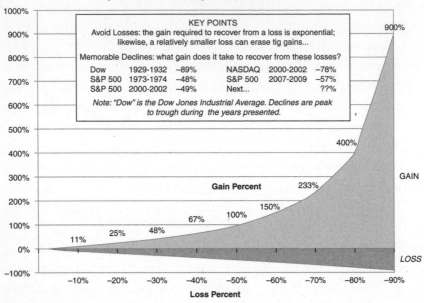

FIGURE 11.4 Avoid Losses

Source: Copyright 2009, Crestmont Research (www.CrestmontResearch.com).

advance. Over an investing period of about 20 years, missing the 10 best days would cost you about half of your capital gains.

However, successfully avoiding the 10 worst days would have an even bigger positive impact: you would have ended up with 2.5. Figure 11.5 shows the importance of missing the 10 worst days from 1981 through 2011.

If we extend the time frame and look at $1,000 invested on January 3, 1950, using a buy-and-hold strategy, the investment would have turned into $8,179 by July 31, 2012. However, if you missed the top 10 best days, you would have only $3,895 instead of $8,179.

If you happened to be very fortunate and missed the 10 worst days in the market during this time frame, your $1,000 would have appreciated to $21,441. Clearly, missing the 10 worst days in the market has a much larger influence on your returns than capturing the 10 best days.

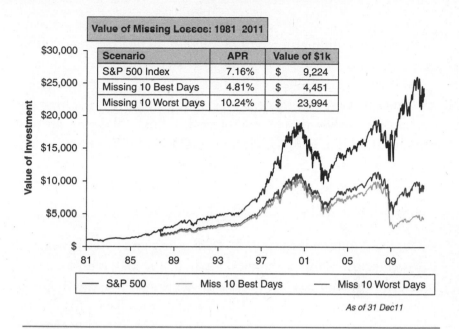

Value of Missing Losses: 1981 2011		
Scenario	APR	Value of $1k
S&P 500 Index	7.16%	$ 9,224
Missing 10 Best Days	4.81%	$ 4,451
Missing 10 Worst Days	10.24%	$ 23,994

As of 31 Dec11

FIGURE 11.5 Missing the 10 Worst Days Is More Important Than Missing the 10 Best Days

Source: Bloomberg, internal.

The reality is that it is unlikely you will catch the 10 best days and miss the 10 worst days. In fact, the 10 best days and 10 worst days often occur in proximity to each other during bear markets. A hallmark of bear markets is high volatility.

So what is the result of missing the top 10 and bottom 10 trading days? The $1,000 initial investment would have grown to $10,294, almost 26 percent higher than it would with the buy-and-hold strategy. Not only would your absolute return have been higher, the portfolio would have experienced lower volatility and the risk-adjusted return would be substantially better. Your life would not have been held hostage by market uncertainty. The argument used to justify a buy-and-hold strategy to capture the 10 best days in the market just does not add up.

Modern portfolio theory has been a straitjacket keeping investors fully invested in stocks no matter how high they go or what is going on in the economy. Investors have been scared out of trying to time the market. Market timing is all about risk management. The risk one is attempting to mitigate with market timing is a life-changing loss.

Many financial advisors structure clients' investment plans in a manner that exposes them to major market downturns. Because advisors often follow the concepts of modern financial theory, including buy and hold, and assume a normal distribution of expected returns and diversification based on predictable correlation, their clients often make modest gains in most years only to occasionally suffer such heavy losses that the years of previous gains are inconsequential.

Buy and hold with proper diversification and asset allocation has become the industry-standard method of retail money management. When you meet with financial advisors, they usually show you a pie chart of asset class allocation after they have talked with you about your investment profile and interests. The pie chart is essentially their recommended allocation of your portfolio between bonds and stocks. Within bonds and stocks, there is likely to be an international slice. Occasionally, your pie might have a slice labeled "alternative" that could include real estate or stock/bond/precious metals blend funds and the like. How the pie slices are cut will be based on your risk tolerance. If you like risk, they will cut you a big piece of equity. If you don't like risk, you will get an extra serving of bonds.

After you agree to your custom pie, your money is segmented and allocated to the various slices. It is highly likely that your pie consists mainly of financial products on the financial advisor's "platform." It is probable that the fees the advisor is paid for serving certain slices of pie have an influence on your pie. The end result of your pie-picking contest is that (1) it is highly unlikely that you have an optimized market portfolio and (2) you are in a buy-and-hold mode until your account receives a modest rebalancing periodically.

You have mixed market timing with buy and hold in the most unfortunate manner. It is unlikely that you are an owner of the market portfolio, meaning you are market timing by underweighting and overweighting sectors relative to the benchmark. Also, you are holding on to your nonoptimized positions through good times and bad times and suffering from whatever the market is dishing out. This is a formula almost certain to lead to underperformance, especially when fees are tacked on.

Part of the reason investors are in this predicament is institutional structural distortions. Some of the most severe distortions are a result of the way financial products are sold. They go through gated networks involving incentive fees and style boxes. Much of the time, the people advising you to buy certain funds really do not understand what they are selling fundamentally. However, they almost always understand what they are selling from an incentive compensation perspective.

A second reason investors are being subjected to such poor advice is legal liability. When you go to see your doctor, you expect that he or she will provide you with at least industry-standard care. If you have ill health and discover the problem could have been prevented by a simple test that is commonly administered, you are likely to sue the doctor if you did not receive the test. This is why doctors perform lots of medical tests even if the tests may not be necessary. It also underlies the fundamental reason financial advisors provide investors with advice that may not be optimal for the client. It is the industry standard.

Financial managers have a fiduciary responsibility to provide you with what is considered appropriate counsel in accordance with your risk tolerance and financial condition. If they provide you with what everyone else in the business is doing, they have at least given you the industry standard. When your results are just like everyone else's, they have done their job and you will probably pay them their fees for the long term. It is safer for a financial advisor to watch you lose your money in a well-diversified, industry-standard portfolio in a major down market than to risk losing you as a customer by attempting to time the market.

The reality is that you normally would not want your financial advisor to attempt to aggressively move your money in and out of the market. Risk management cannot be based on intuition. It should be disciplined and systematic. It must leave no opening for emotion to take control. Very few financial advisors have a proven system in place for managing money through value-added market timing. This is usually not the common method for managing risk.

We know plenty of money managers who definitely felt the coming weakness in early 2008, but without a specific mechanism to help make actual market timing decisions, most took little or no action. The investment world is filled with clutter, including endless media attention to sensational headlines that can bias or paralyze decision making. Market timing becomes even harder as a sell-off intensifies. To sell after a 10 percent decline is hard. Selling is even harder after a 20 percent or 30 percent drop. Without a systematic way to manage risk, buy and hold is easy and accepted and is offered as the industry standard.

A famous Wall Street adage is that the financial markets are designed to inflict the largest amount of pain on the largest amount of people at any point in time. For example, at the Nasdaq peak in 2000, individuals could not get into technology stocks fast enough. This was just in time for an 80 percent Nasdaq market collapse. After the U.S. stock market bottom in March 2009, individuals pulled money out of equities and invested in bonds at a record pace. Whereas bonds have had a tremendous run since 2009, equities advanced by more than 100 percent over the next several years. It would not be crazy to predict that by the time the bond market has attracted a large percentage of everyone's money and is wildly overcrowded, interest rates may trend higher and investors will once again be hit by a significant decline in a major portion of their portfolios.

Many bond experts, including Bill Gross, cofounder of PIMCO, the largest bond management firm in the world, are not enthusiastic about the secular bull case for bonds. What worries bond managers today is that interest rates are near all-time lows after declining on a secular basis for 30 years and governments have huge incentives to stimulate inflation as a way to "reflate" the economy and diminish the existing debt liability in real terms. Bonds respond inversely to their interest rates. If interest rates begin to rise on a secular basis, bond prices will fall. If you believe in the mantra of buy low, sell high, it does not take much imagination to believe that bond values are at risk as a result of rising rates over the next decade.

Figure 11.6 shows the decline in 10-year U.S. Treasury yields from their peak in 1982 through 2012.

In the wake of the 2008–2009 credit crisis, many investors sought refuge and yield in the municipal bond market. Municipal bonds, long considered safe investments, "actually go bad much more than we thought," says Karen Weise in Businessweek.com. Many municipal bonds are not graded by the big ratings agencies, Moody's and Standard & Poor's. In examining muni defaults, researchers at the Federal Reserve Bank of New York included unrated bonds and found 2,521 defaults from 1970 to 2011—35 times more than in those tracked by Moody's.

In the early 1980s, there was a debt crisis in Latin America in which the foreign debt owed by many Latin American countries was substantially larger than their earnings power and they defaulted.

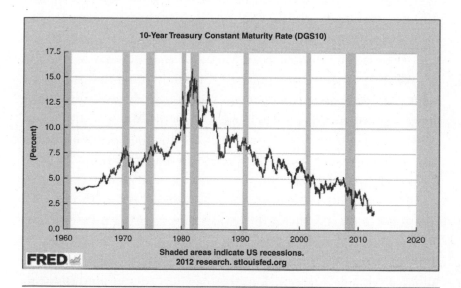

FIGURE 11.6 Ten-Year U.S. Treasury Yields, 1960–2012

Source: Board of Governors of the Federal Reserve System.

The losses sustained by the large American banks from their exposure to the Latin American debt crisis wiped out almost all of the cumulative profits of the banks up to that point. After defaulting in 1982, Latin America essentially lost a decade of economic advancement and did not begin to recover until 1992. With our own credit crisis and the European debt crisis not fully played out, the lesson from the Latin American debt crisis is that the U.S. stock market could experience continued turbulence for several more years.

Whether you are investing in bonds or stocks, investing involves risk. You buy insurance on your home, health, and car. You buy insurance because you cannot predict the future with certainty. Why would you not take out an insurance policy on your liquid assets as well? If we know a wide array of possible outcomes may occur, we can be sure that over time, there is a high probability that some of these outcomes will be negative. Most people have no plan for this other than diversification and time. Unfortunately, we know diversification has not been a robust insurance policy, and many of us just don't have the time.

Traders who manage their portfolios with some form of insurance and a high awareness of the "fat tail" event survive. Insurance gives them the ability to remove some anxiety from the process of investing. These traders are able to sleep at night knowing they have a plan for avoiding a major down market. They understand that it does not matter if a positive outcome occurs with a high degree of frequency if the negative outcome is completely unacceptable.

People like to say that these times are different and the world is about to "normalize." Some investors believe that with the S&P 500 having experienced a drawdown of more than 50 percent during the credit crisis, it is unlikely that such a severe sell-off will happen for a number of years. What if the reality is that a major market sell-off increases the chances of experiencing another major market sell-off in the near term? When you look at the market passing through supercycles, it becomes obvious that bad occurrences tend to cluster during certain long phases of market history.

This book is about having a nonemotional, systematic, proven plan for participating in up markets and applying risk controls for staying out of major down markets. It is about having an insurance policy against suffering from the wealth-destroying effects of a major down market.

CHAPTER TWELVE

A History of Mutual Funds and the Story of Jeffrey Vinik

THE FIRST open-end mutual fund, Massachusetts Investors Trust, began on March 21, 1924. For the first 30 years, the industry grew at a slow pace. It was not until 1951 that the number of funds exceeded 100. When you compare this to the early history of the exchange-traded fund (ETF) industry, it is unbelievably slow. The first ETF traded on the American Stock Exchange in 1993. At the end of 2000, there were 80 ETFs. From 2000 to 2010, ETF assets under management grew by more than 30 percent per year. In 2012, ETFs had $1.2 trillion in assets held in 1,476 funds and account for nearly one-third of U.S. equity trading (*Barron's* Special Report, *The New ETF Handbook*, July 16, 2012).

During the 1950s, mutual fund asset accumulation began to accelerate, and by the end of the decade, total mutual fund holdings were about $15.8 billion. In 1976, John C. Bogle opened the first retail index fund, the First Index Investment Trust (the Vanguard 500 Index Fund). Bogle was providing investors with a tangible way to implement a buy-and-hold strategy of the market portfolio for a low fee. In 1977, Peter Lynch took over the Fidelity Magellan Fund, the nation's premier actively managed fund. By 1980, mutual fund assets were roughly $95 billion and had grown 9.3 percent per annum for 20 years. The growth rate would nearly double to 17.4 percent over the next 30 years.

The 401(k) plan—named for a section of the Internal Revenue Code—was created by Congress in 1978. By 1980, companies had begun the steady process of replacing pension plans with far less costly 401(k) plans. In 1981, Congress created the individual retirement account (IRA). The twin creations of the 401(k) and the IRA really lit the fire of growth, and by the end of the 1980s, there were 8,200 mutual funds with almost $7 trillion under management. Millions of Americans were having a regular portion of their pay diverted every month into mutual funds via their 401(k) and IRA savings plans. The Investment Company Institute estimates that the U.S. mutual fund industry had a collective $11.6 trillion held in roughly 8,684 funds as of 2011.

Mutual fund assets are highly concentrated in the largest fund companies. The largest 5 mutual fund companies hold 40 percent of the assets, the largest 10 hold 53 percent, and the largest 25 hold 73 percent. The trend towards a concentration of assets in the largest firms has been steady over the last decade.

During the bull run of 1982–2000, mutual funds began to replace banks as the repository of Americans' wealth. Big fund companies such as Fidelity morphed from being innovative and aggressive into acting more like a public utility in the minds of many Americans. Dependability and predictability became the key operating parameters.

Figure 12.1 shows the share of household assets held in investment companies. From 1980 through 2011, the share rose from 3 percent to 23 percent. By the end of 2011, investment companies held 29 percent of the outstanding stock in the United States.

Because they represent roughly half of all the value of retirement plans, the way mutual funds invest is a major driver of stock behavior and offers some insight into the types of risk investors are being exposed to when they buy a mutual fund.

Jeffrey Vinik managed the Fidelity Magellan Fund, the world's best known actively managed mutual fund, from 1992 to May 23, 1996.

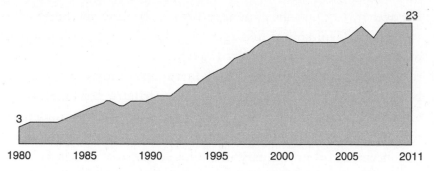

Note: Household financial assets held in registered investment companies include household holdings of ETFs, closed-end funds, UITs, and mutual funds. Mutual funds held in employer-sponsored DC plans, IRAs, and variable annuities are included.

The next two charts show the percentage of mutual funds in household retirement accounts.

Mutual fund Percentage of Retirement Assets by Type of Retirement Vehicle 1991-2011

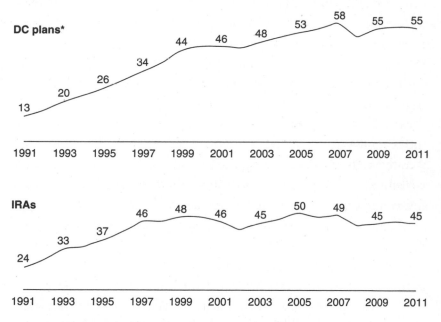

* DC plans include 403(b) plans, 457 plans, and private employer-sponsored DC plans (including 401(k) plans).

FIGURE 12.1 Household Financial Assets Held in Registered Investment Companies; 3 percent Grows to 23 percent, 1980–2011

Source: Investment Company Institute and Federal Reserve Board.

He averaged 17 percent annual returns, outpacing the S&P 500's 11.6 percent. Unlike star manager Peter Lynch, who applied a bottom-up investment style and liked to talk about buying companies he had personal familiarity with, Vinik first applied a top-down analysis before using a bottom-up approach to pick specific stocks. Like George Chestnutt, Vinik believed that picking a good stock in an underperforming industry would lead to disappointing returns. Vinik chose to concentrate his investments in market sectors that he felt had tailwinds. Whereas Lynch carried an average of 1,400 separate stocks in the fund, Vinik used fewer than 475 stocks in 1995.

Lynch was seemingly a tough act to follow. During his 13-year term as the fund manager, he earned an average annual return of 26.4 percent, nearly double the S&P 500 return of 13.3 percent. At least that is what the headlines said. The reality is that the Magellan fund was an incubator fund that was open only to Fidelity employees until 1981. It turns out that the average non–Fidelity employee investor earned an average annual return of 13.4 percent from 1981 to 1990, trailing the S&P 500's 16.2 percent return.

The initial success of the fund occurred when the asset base was roughly $100 million. As the asset base moved into the billions and the fund began to own 1,400 stocks, Magellan was essentially a closet index fund with high fees. In 1990, at the age of 46, Lynch retired a wealthy man. He then leveraged his fame and added to his wealth by writing three books: *One Up on Wall Street, Beating the Street,* and *Learn to Earn.*

As a point of historical interest, Lynch was initially hired as an intern by Fidelity Investments in 1966 partly because he had been caddying for Fidelity's president at Brae Burn Country Club in Newton, Massachusetts. What is funny about this is that no one can remember the name of the former Fidelity president but many investors know who the former caddy is.

Vinik, by deviating substantially from the Lynch style of investing and the market portfolio, was engaged in active market timing. Vinik recognized that owning a good house in a bad neighborhood was not nearly as attractive an investment as owning a bad house in a good neighborhood. The overall health of the sector and the market has a tremendous effect on the performance of a specific stock pick.

As Vinik moved away from holding a broad array of stocks, his returns were more likely to deviate from the major index benchmarks. Fidelity's management perceived this style to be inconsistent with the investment objectives of its client base. Money was flowing into the Fidelity Magellan Fund because investors expected market consistent risk (standard deviation) with at least market returns. Vinik's approach potentially increased return volatility and exposed the fund to substantially worse than market expected returns for periods of time.

In 1995, Vinik's return was 36.8 percent versus the S&P 500 return of 37.6 percent. Investors were upset at the end of the year when he underperformed by the tiny amount of 0.8 percent. In December 1995, Vinik made a job-ending market timing decision. He moved 32 percent of Magellan's $50 billion fund into cash and bonds. Additionally, he reduced the technology stock holdings of the fund from 43.2 percent at the end of October 1995 to 8.4 percent in December. His timing could not have been worse. Interest rates jumped higher, hurting his bond holdings, and technology stocks went on a bull run. By the end of May, Vinik was no longer working at Fidelity.

If the stock market had corrected as Vinik believed it would, Fidelity would have labeled him a market mastermind willing to take the necessary risks to lead the pack. Over the four years Vinik ran the fund, his cumulative return of 83.7 percent outperformed the cumulative S&P 500 return by 5.91 percent. His legacy, however, was to strongly reaffirm the practice of mutual funds investing like closet index funds. Funds that delivered average returns did not lose assets. Funds that strayed far from the benchmark investment profiles were at high risk of having investors take their money elsewhere.

The story of Jeffrey Vinik had a tremendous impact on the mutual fund industry. He was a highly respected investment superstar managing the premier American mutual fund. His departure from Fidelity sent a loud and clear message to the rest of the industry: stray from buy and hold at your own risk.

After leaving Fidelity, Vinik founded Vinik Asset Management. In his first 11 months, the fund was up 93.8 percent. For the next three years, his average annual return was roughly 50 percent. At the end of 2000, he returned his investors' money (roughly $4.2 billion) and focused on managing his own portfolio. He is the current owner of the Tampa Bay Lightning (NHL) and the Tampa Bay Storm (AFL) as well as a minority owner of the Boston Red Sox (MLB).

It turns out that Vinik really is a talented money manager who would have served Fidelity clients well if he had been allowed to stay the course. Unfortunately for all of us, this extraordinarily talented active manager was turned into a poster boy for why market timing does not work and why investors should adopt a buy-and-hold equity approach.

From 1990 through June 2010, Magellan earned 7.8 percent annually, lagging the S&P 500 by 0.4 percent per year. For those who seek quality active managers today, their primary access is through hedge funds, which normally have high fees, lockups, and low transparency and allow only wealthy (accredited) investors to participate. Most of the major mutual funds attempt to mirror their benchmarks. Fund management teams see their primary objective as staying close to their benchmarks rather than protecting your money from a major market downturn.

CHAPTER THIRTEEN

Paradigm Shift

a. Shift One: The Buy-and-Hold Era

From the day humankind began trading in marketplaces until about the 1970s, active trading was considered standard operating procedure. If you had advised people in the 1930s that buy and hold was the best approach to building wealth through stock ownership, they would have said you were crazy. It was completely obvious to most people that there are boom and bust cycles and that you could make a fortune during boom times and lose it all during the busts. Most rational investors intuitively understand the concept of making every effort to limit exposure to severe market declines.

By the 1970s, a harmonic convergence of events had occurred to bring about the nearly universal acceptance that buy and hold is the optimum method for investment. In buy-and-hold investing, it is implied that when you buy has a decreasing impact on returns as the investment horizon extends. Whether an investor buys the market when it is wildly overvalued (Nasdaq at 5,000) or is at its trough, over time it will have an inconsequential effect on expected returns. Although it is evident today that this thinking is misguided mostly because valuation differentials have been substantial and it does not fit most people's investment time parameters, for over three decades it was the industry standard.

Markowitz, Sharpe, Samuelson, and other financial economists began to dominate the thinking about investment theory in the 1950s, 1960s, and 1970s. As academic theory coalesced around buy and hold, an increasing number of young finance and economic graduates entered the workplace convinced that modern portfolio theory prescribed the optimum way to invest. Many of those graduates reached their prime years of influence just in time to catch the largest bull market in modern history, from 1982 to 2000. Over the entire stretch from 1970 through 2009, according to StandardandPoors.com, the S&P 500 return was 10.1 percent annually, including dividends. Any theory that said you should buy and hold stocks during a time when the stock market was essentially doubling every seven years would have been well received. Buy and hold was highly attractive, easy, and tax-efficient and was perceived as the responsible way to invest by the experts.

On May 1, 1975, the SEC abolished the fixed commissions that had kept the cost of stock trading in the stratosphere. Historically, brokerage houses were predominantly focused on institutions and wealthy individuals. Almost everyone else had disadvantaged access to the stock market. After "May Day" and for the first time in 180 years, trading fees were set by market competition. The deregulation of commissions opened the doors to a new industry—the discount brokerage—in which individual self-directed investors traded securities without a stockbroker. Stockbrokers, paid with trading commissions and prodded by investment bank research, often viewed active management as the best way to manage portfolios. Individuals, who now had access to the stock market through firms such as Charles Schwab (founded in 1975), focused on trading costs, which could be minimized with a buy-and-hold approach.

The laws creating the IRA and 401(k) plans helped make Wall Street more accessible to Main Street but also helped create the passive investor. Active company pension managers were being replaced by individuals who did not have the training necessary to be active. The investment opportunity set offered to most individuals through their 401(k) plans featured buy-and-hold-type investments. Investors, by making regular monthly contributions, were making no attempt to time the market. The phrase *dollar cost averaging* was used to describe these regular buying patterns. Many individuals whose

401(k) contributions were withdrawn from their paychecks automatically were hardly aware that their money was flowing into stocks monthly. With the market rising on a regular basis, there was no pressure to overthink the possible risks associated with stock market investing, particularly if the investing was for a long-term purpose such as retirement.

Stocks were selling at rock bottom valuations in the middle and late 1970s. The price/earnings multiple on the S&P 500 was a single digit. When stocks are at their low, the expected 10-year annualized return is roughly 15 percent. Ironically, although investors had been told to ignore stock valuations and just keep buying and holding, the beginning of the bull cycle was matched with a low in stock valuations. As Warren Greene says, "the best way to have a successful mutual fund is to open it at a market low."

About 76 million American children were born between 1945 and 1964. The first of those baby boomers were just reaching their prime investment years in 1982. At the end of the 1960s, only 15 percent of households held stock market investments. With the confluence of the 401(k)/IRA investment vehicles in the 1970s and the conviction that stocks offered the best long-term returns, increasing numbers of boomers directed their savings into stocks. By 1995 more than half of U.S. households owned equity. This new generation of investors was far removed from the scars left by the Great Depression of the 1930s.

Many investors, especially those with larger accounts, use the services of investment advisors. ICI research finds that among investors owning mutual fund shares outside of retirement plans at work, 80 percent own fund shares through financial professionals. These investment professionals tend to be asset allocators as opposed to active managers. Under their oversight, the equity allocation of client portfolios is almost always placed in a buy-and-hold mode.

Within the mutual fund companies themselves, management was increasingly becoming focused on matching market returns rather than exceeding them. Vinik's experience helped consolidate industry thinking around fee collection over outperformance. Big fund management is generally risk-averse. If the fund manager is being paid to manage equities, the fund is expected to stay in equities. Vinik's huge tactical asset allocation decisions are essentially unheard of today in most mutual funds. In the short term, Vinik's market timing decisions were poorly timed. He missed an important bullish stock move, and his bonds were hit by rising interest rates. Generally, fund managements cannot reasonably explain to their investors why they are not in stocks when stocks appreciate. If the cost of retaining investors in a mutual fund is being locked into stocks and riding the big moves down, so be it.

Retail investors usually do not withdraw money from their mutual funds as long as the funds perform about as well as the overall market. From a fund company's standpoint, the endgame is to build assets under management (AUM) and charge fees. It is a lot easier and safer to perform about as well as the benchmark indexes and run a strong marketing department with solid customer service than it is to attempt to outperform the market consistently and attract assets through fund performance. This is especially true as AUM migrates up into the billions and trillions of dollars and the funds are forced to buy thousands of stocks just to put the money to work.

Once you own tens of stocks, let alone hundreds and thousands, the performance of your portfolio will not deviate much from that of the broad market. Studies have shown that if you pick 18 stocks randomly, you have achieved about 90 percent of the benefit of diversification. If you are not completely random in your stock selection, a group of 20 to 30 stocks tends to remove 70 percent of the risk that your performance will deviate much from the market.

Mutual fund portfolio managers who control billions of dollars are not able to know their stock holdings well. There are just too many of them. These funds bring little competitive insight into the ownership of most of their holdings. As an investor, you are in effect paying active management fees for passive ownership.

Funds flow into mutual funds from sales that rely on style boxes, as shown in Figure 13.1.

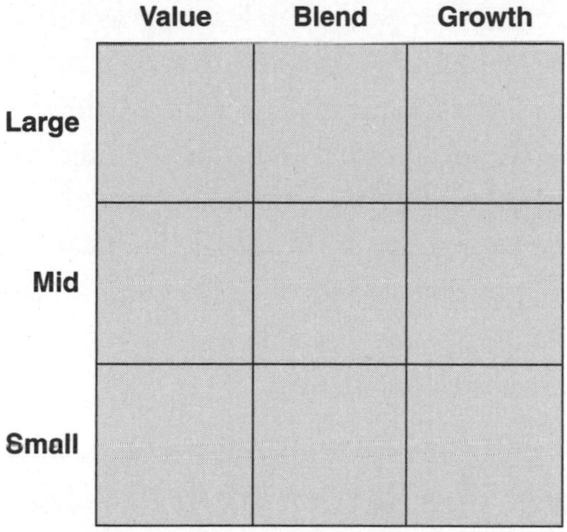

	Value	Blend	Growth
Large			
Mid			
Small			

FIGURE 13.1 Style Boxes

The term *style boxes* is used to describe funds with labels such as large cap value, small cap aggressive growth, and so on. Style boxes allow funds to be reviewed relative to their category of investment style. These styles are somewhat rigidly defined. If a fund does not fit a predefined style box, it will struggle in the distribution channel and is unlikely to build AUM. Since the endgame is to build AUM, mutual funds generally do not stray outside their style boxes. In fact, funds are evaluated on what is called style drift and negatively scored as a result of such drift.

Demographics, IRAs, 401(k)s, the 20-year bull market, academic theory, style boxes, and the sheer size of the industry have conspired to freeze much of the retail investment world in a buy-and-hold approach. Because many funds are poorly indexed and carry fees, the industry as a whole has underperformed the market. Studies have shown that the average active mutual fund over the last couple of decades has a negative alpha of 1.15 percent. This means the average mutual fund has underperformed its investment-style benchmark by 1.15 percent per year. More important, investors who believed stock diversification was all the risk management they needed have been rudely awakened by the Nasdaq bubble burst and the credit crisis since 2000.

Action—reaction. The pendulum is swinging the other way. Investors are wondering how it was possible that their mutual fund portfolio managers and investment advisors let them down so badly during the 2008–2009 financial crisis. They are no longer willing to accept buy and hold as gospel. Investors want and need their money to work for them. If they are going to ride in the boat called stocks, they at least want a life preserver. Many who have lost all confidence in the boat would like to get out of the boat entirely. They seek absolute returns rather than relative returns.

b. Shift Two: The Return of Active Management

The bursting of the dot-com and tech stock bubbles in 2000–2002 was the first major alert in the last 25 years that buy and hold may not be the best strategy for all market cycles. The 2008–2009 credit crisis pounded this point home for those who were not paying close attention. Between June 2005 and June 2010, the S&P 500 index dropped 10.4 percent, and between June 2000 and June 2010, it tumbled 26.0 percent.

As of July 2012, the average holding period for the S&P 500 SPDR (SPY), one of the ETFs that track the S&P 500, was less than five days according to Alan Newman's *Crosscurrents* newsletter, as quoted on CNBC. The entire capitalization of the SPY turns over at least once per week. Much of this is caused by institutional trading, but it does suggest that the world is moving away from a buy-and-hold approach.

In 1997, hedge funds controlled roughly $100 billion of actively managed funds. Today, hedge funds have AUM of approximately $1.7 trillion and funds of funds control another $555 billion. Figure 13.2 shows the growth of hedge fund (HF) assets from 1997 through 2010. On the left-hand *y* axis, you can see hedge fund assets as a percentage of global equity markets, and on the right, the total assets under management in billions of dollars. In a nutshell, during a time when fund flows have been away from equities generally, hedge funds have been seeing inflows and gaining market share.

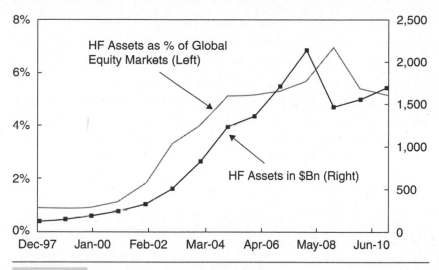

FIGURE 13.2 **Hedge Fund Asset Growth, 1997–2010**

Source: JPMorgan Equity Derivatives Strategy, BarclayHedge LTD—Alternate Investments database.

Hedge funds are all about active management. Their purpose is to figure out (1) when to buy, (2) what to buy, and (3) when to sell. This is pure market timing. Many hedge funds are engaged in short-term trading and incur high rates of portfolio turnover.

Because hedge funds engage in frequent trading, they generate a disproportionate amount of trade commissions relative to their assets under management. As a result, investment bank sales and trading teams focus on hedge fund clients as a top priority. Hedge fund performance benefits from getting the first call from the sell-side research or sales team. Partly because of their information advantage, many highly visible, aggressive, multi-billion-dollar hedge funds have posted significant outperformance for years.

The endowments of Yale, Stanford, Princeton, and Harvard have relied on alternative investing and hedge funds for years. These institutions were some of the first to recognize the importance of finding funds that perform like equities in up markets but provide strong downside protection in bearish markets. Because of the investment success of these endowments, many investors look to imitate their investment methodology. In 2007, PIMCO, a global investment management firm with roughly $1.8 trillion under management, hired the former CEO of Harvard Management Company, Mohamed A. El-Erian, as co-chief investment officer for a compensation package of roughly $100 million per year.

The growth of hedge fund assets is indicative of a growing interest in active management versus buy and hold. The problem for most retail investors is that hedge funds are not an accessible investment vehicle. To invest in a hedge fund, you usually have to be an accredited investor: "a natural person who has individual net worth, or joint net worth with the person's spouse, that exceeds $1 million at the time of the purchase, excluding the value of the primary residence of such person or a natural person with income exceeding $200,000 in each of the two most recent years or joint income with a spouse exceeding $300,000 for those years and a reasonable expectation of the same income level in the current year" (SEC).

In addition to being available only to institutional or high-net-worth investors, hedge funds lack transparency, restrict investors' access to their money, and charge incredibly high fees. Many describe hedge funds as a compensation plan rather than an investment strategy. Hedge funds often charge a fee of 2 percent on all assets under management and a performance fee of 20 percent of all profits. The more successful funds charge even more.

A growing number of retail money management firms are beginning to offer investors active management strategies that involve transitioning money between asset classes to capture equitylike returns with a focus on down market avoidance. The problem with many of these offerings is they were formed after 2009 and have not been tested over time by a wide variety of market conditions.

Active trading has benefited from a tremendous decline in trading costs. It used to be that the "friction" of trading including wide bid–ask spreads and high commissions served as a deterrent to rapid position changes. Before April 9, 2001, stocks were quoted in fractions denominated in increments of one-sixteenth (1/16). Before 1997, stocks were quoted in increments of one-eighth (1/8) or a minimum spread of 12.5 cents. Legend has it that the 1/8 system originated with

Spanish traders counting their doubloons on eight fingers (thumbs did not count). Today, spreads can be a penny or less with what is known as decimalization.

Combined with the tightening of spreads has been the severe compression of commissions. Until the early 1970s stocks traded on a fixed commission set by the NYSE, up to 2 percent each way (or 4 percent in and out) of the total value of the shares being traded, with extra fees for smaller transactions sometimes doubling the cost. In dollars, 100,000 shares of a $20 stock created a $40,000 commission one-way. By 1996, the commission had dropped to $6,000. By 2012, the same order could be done for a commission of roughly $300.

The ease of trading has skyrocketed. Discount brokerage firms now offer free market data feeds and quote systems, sophisticated electronic order entry, and online account viewing. Order executions often take place in milliseconds rather than minutes, allowing traders to have higher confidence that orders will be filled at the price they see on their screens. Investment vehicles such as ETFs have facilitated investors' ability to act on trade ideas rapidly and with less stock-specific risk. Inverse mutual funds and inverse ETFs encourage active management as it allows investors to play both the up and the down fluctuations of the market. Essentially, active management today is cheap and easy when it comes to execution. Getting in and out of the market involves only the push of a button.

In 1960, the average holding period for stocks was 100 months (eight years) according to the NYSE *Fact Book*. In 2010, the average holding period had dropped to six months. With the ease, low price, and wide availability of trading products to facilitate active stock management and with the promise of higher returns than buy and hold, it is evident that a paradigm shift to market timing and tactical trading is under way. This trend is even more impressive when you consider the headwinds presented by taxes that provide an incentive for investors to hold stocks for at least one year. Short-term stock market gains are taxed at regular income rates, whereas long-term gains are taxed at 15 percent currently.

Over the last several years, the financial media have increasingly talked about the risk-on/risk-off trade. Risk-off lately has generally meant a rush to buy U.S. Treasuries as the viability of the euro and the possibility of a euro zone sovereign debt default have increased. Risk-on has meant money coming out of Treasuries and into stocks. Risk-on/risk-off trades can take all kinds of forms in a wide variety of securities. However it is conducted, it represents a recognition by investors that safety is a priority and active trading is a necessity.

Ironically, we ended our phone conversation with Warren Greene, president of the No Load Mutual Fund Association from 1977 to 1979, because he had to jump to execute a trade in his personal account. Who says you can't teach an old dog new tricks?

CHAPTER FOURTEEN

The Story of Neil Peplinski and Good Harbor

THE PEPLINSKIS were northern Michigan dairy farmers. Like many dairy farmers in that area, their days were filled with milking cows, planting hay, and picking rocks out of the fields. As is the case with most farm work, more hands are better to help carry the load. Neil Peplinski was the youngest of seven siblings.

Farming had positive effects on Neil. He learned about getting up before sunrise and working hard. He learned about taking a simple, straightforward approach to life. Neil's approach to life is almost exactly what you would expect in the son of a dairy farmer: direct, want-to-see-for-myself, and devoid of preconceived notions. As a young man, he favored situations that were analytical, systematic, understandable and, most of all, reliable.

Farming taught Neil about market risk. The Peplinskis lived at the mercy of milk price volatility. There was no commodity futures contract they could trade to hedge away the risk of falling milk prices. Liquid milk futures did not begin to trade until the late 1990s. The monetary rewards for a hard day of dairy farming were controlled by factors way beyond the horizons of the Peplinski farm. During Neil's childhood, being a dairy farmer was a buy-and-hold proposition. At some basic level, Neil was learning that there are times when you want to be a dairy farmer and times when you don't.

Neil was comfortable with numbers. He always did well academically, particularly in science and math. His desire to move away from dairy farming and his satisfaction and comfort with math led him to sell his prized grand champion steer and pay for his first year at Michigan Technological University. Four years later, Neil graduated summa cum laude with a bachelor of science in electrical engineering in electromagnetics. With his ease with numbers and academic success, Neil took the next step and earned a master of science in electrical engineering in electromagnetics from the University of Michigan.

Neil was able to secure a position in Motorola's cellular infrastructure group in 1994. As a top-notch engineer, he made a living performing data analysis to optimize performance. No one likes a dropped cell phone call. Rather than working in the open fields with cows, hay, and rocks, Neil was now in a gray cubicle, sitting under fireproof white ceiling tiles and using stochastic calculus and Fourier transformations to convert data from the time domain to the frequency domain. Motorola was the technology leader in mobile communications as cell phones were undergoing explosive, geometric growth in the 1990s.

As many of us know, part of living modern corporate life inside a cubicle involves the challenge of navigating the company 401(k) program. Most of us skim through the performance histories of the various investment options and then elect to put our money to work in what seems like the best programs at the moment before forgetting about it until the company asks us to rethink our investment selections annually. For Neil, who had no previous exposure to stock market investing and a penchant for numbers, the 401(k) looked like just another opportunity for an engineering adventure.

Neil saw picking 401(k) investment alternatives as just another optimization problem. He understood that if he held money in a buy-and-hold stock fund, there was a good chance that his portfolio would experience a major drawdown at some point. From the standpoint of portfolio performance optimization, Neil began the process of analyzing how to determine when it is time to transition entirely out of stocks to avoid major bearish markets.

Neil loaded over 100 years of market data into his computers. He then subjected the data to conversions between the time and frequency domains. He treated stock market data just as he would electromagnetic cell phone and base station data with a full-on torture test involving stochastic calculus. His data-driven analytical mind was looking for optimization. He was thinking outside the box because this former dairy farmer did not know there was a box when it came to financial theory and stock market investing.

As Neil stared at the data, he could not get comfortable with the idea of owning stocks all the time. He heard fellow employees say he should just buy stocks. Neil was young, and stocks had the best long-term appreciation record. They always came back from a major sell-off over time. This was the mid–1990s, 15 years into a bull market supercycle. In bullish supercycles, buying on the dips works because the market is in an appreciating trend. What Neil noticed in the data, however, is that there are long periods—15 to 25 years—when stock prices are flat to down. Because Neil recognized that he was unlikely to live for 200 years, extended down market cycles caught his attention as a risk that should not be ignored. As in dairy farming, there are times you want to be involved with the market and times you don't.

From 1994 through 2000, people became addicted to using cell phones. Motorola was a market leader, which the stock market recognized by lifting the stock from about $60 to roughly $225, a nearly 300 percent increase. For most Motorola employees, investing the 401(k) did not seem to require much engineering talent. All you had to do was buy Motorola stock.

Neil could not separate himself from the data. The data kept telling him that markets do not go up forever. He knew that being in a down market was a much bigger risk than missing a major up market. He was uncomfortable with being a market-beating stock picker as the data said this was hard to do consistently over time. Neil was more interested in owning stocks during bullish market cycles and not owning them in bearish cycles. His primary risk management concern was not tied up with what stocks to own; it was all about not owning any stocks during bear markets.

Because Neil understood farming and the problem of fluctuating farm commodity prices such as the price of milk, his first look at securities trading was in the world of farm commodity futures. He intuitively understood this market. He knew that it is part of human nature for people's willingness to take on risk exposure changes over time. During good times, people are willing to extend themselves and put more money at risk. On the farm, this might translate into buying new equipment. During times of crisis, people draw back and are highly risk-averse. To protect themselves, they hold on to every penny. Without knowing it at the time, Neil was moving in exactly the opposite direction of the prevailing economic theory, which assumed that the expected risk premium for owning stocks is a constant.

As an engineer, Neil realized that if he could somehow measure changes in risk perceptions, he would have a way to systematically and reliably know when to be in or out of stocks. Farmer Neil had planted the seeds of the next chapter in his life.

He was now an engineering manager at Motorola, and his 401(k) had grown. Rather than pick individual stocks, Neil was using the equity and debt index-based ETF products offered through Motorola's 401(k) program to control his equity market exposure. He was actively managing his 401(k) and posting his results for other Motorola engineers to see. Every month, Neil would make disciplined, data-based analytic decisions about whether to be in stocks. If risk perceptions were rising, Neil was entirely out of stocks. If risk perceptions were falling, he was 100 percent in stocks. Neil was not afraid to act on the data. In fact, for a data guy, that came rather easily.

From high to low, Motorola stock dropped from about $225 into the mid-$20s during the Nasdaq bubble bust (March 2000 to April 2003). Motorola 401(k) plans that were highly exposed to Motorola stock were struck by a nearly 90 percent loss. Many of Neil's Motorola engineer colleagues were technology-heavy, Nasdaq-focused investors. Some of them were down by over 70 percent.

For engineers making only modest raises each year in a high-technology industry in which jobs come and go because of rapid technology product cycles, the blow was devastating. All of a sudden, the idea Neil had been talking about for the last half decade of staying out of major down markets struck home. Neil's analytics and data analysis had been right all along. He had participated in up markets but had used his calculations of changing risk perceptions to sidestep disaster. In 2003, Neil opened an investment firm on the side and started accepting money to manage from Motorola employees who were leaving the company and wanted to roll their 401(k) plans into an IRA.

By 2004, Neil's interest in quantitative finance was on the rise. He wanted to explore this interest more deeply but needed to keep his engineering job at Motorola as he was now married and beginning to build a family with his wife. At night and on weekends from 2004 through 2006, Neil attended classes at the University of Chicago and earned an MBA in analytical finance. Neil graduated with a perfect grade point average and was the valedictorian of the class.

Neil's experience earning an MBA gave him the language used in finance to talk about the concept of changing risk perceptions and its impact on the capital asset pricing model (CAPM) and modern portfolio theory (MPT). Neil could now explain that markets rise and fall because people are willing to have risky assets in their portfolios, and then something changes and they decide they want to have less risky assets. That something, in many cases, was the tech bubble bust and the 2008 credit crisis. Thus, even though projected cash flows may not change materially, the impact of investors collectively buying and selling assets based on a common change in risk perception causes significant changes in value. When investors are selling their risky assets, stocks are headed south.

The University of Chicago MBA gave Neil the framework and tools to rigorously examine his stock management methodology and evaluate it relative to modern finance theory. When he discovered that one of the underlying assumptions embedded in CAPM and MPT is that investors' views toward risk are a constant (don't change), he knew he had found something elementally wrong with the theory. Armed with a quantitative finance degree, he now also had the credibility to be taken seriously when he talked about it.

Beyond the language, credibility, and financial rigor, Neil's greatest asset gained in the Chicago MBA program was the people he met. Neil found a kindred spirit in Professor John Cochrane, who taught a class titled "Markets Are Predictable." It is somewhat ironic that John Cochrane is the son-in-law of the economist Eugene F. Fama, who is known for arguing that it is pointless for investors to attempt to use publicly available information to forecast stock prices as the prices already contain all known information. Eugene Fama is one of the architects of a market belief system that instructs you to take the beatings until morale improves because markets cannot be predicted.

Paul Ingersoll was also a student in the Chicago MBA program. After majoring in economics and French at the University of Michigan, he had spent eight years building an equipment finance company that eventually went public as National Equipment Services (NSV) with 3,500 employees on the New York Stock Exchange. During the three weeks the company was being marketed to institutional investors on the IPO deal road show in 1998, the stock market tanked. The IPO, which was originally planned to raise $300 million of equity, was cut back to a $100 million offering. NSV was born with a fatal flaw: it carried too much debt relative to its equity. By 2004, NSV was bankrupt and Paul was a 37-year-old student at Chicago.

Paul met Neil in a quantitative finance class Neil was helping with as the teacher's assistant. Paul was immediately struck by the fact that Neil, a fellow MBA student, was the TA rather than one of the many PhD students at Chicago. This was extraordinary. Normally, the TA is one of the brightest PhD students.

At the time of graduation, Neil was 34 years old and Paul was 39. Paul felt that he was too old to jump into the typical MBA career track at a consulting, private equity, or investment banking firm and did not have the experience to step directly into a senior management role. He ended up as the CFO of a private equity firm. Right about when Paul started his job, his firm formed a partnership with another firm that had a more senior CFO. This new CFO took one look at Paul and thought that this was not someone he wanted hanging around attempting to take his job. Within a couple of months, the firm let Paul go with a nice cash payment to buy him out of his contract.

Neil found work at Allstate Investments as an analyst. In the fall of 2006 and the first half of 2007, Allstate was buying collateralized debt obligations (CDOs) that were AAA-rated. The securities were paying 75 basis points above Treasuries, and Allstate wanted to know if this yield premium was sufficient compensation for the potential risks involved. No one in-house at Allstate could figure out how to answer this question in a rigorous manner. A year before the credit crisis, CDOs were hot commodities with financial institutions as they carried the highest credit ratings and high relative yields.

Neil built a model that showed the securities were not a good buy. Allstate stopped acquiring CDOs. Less than a year later, the credit crisis hit and CDOs were trading at 5 cents on the dollar.

Allstate immediately made Neil the portfolio manager. This again was unheard of. Neil was about one year out of school. He had no prior portfolio management experience of any size. Although he was a master at managing his 401(k) account and those of a few friends from Motorola, he did not have the pedigree to take on the senior management responsibility for running a $400 million CDO portfolio.

Then Paul called. Paul was now out of a job but had some cash and thought it was time for him and Neil to build a money management firm. In his early forties, Paul had a strong feeling of now or never. Paul was somewhat amazed at how easy it was to talk Neil into leaving Allstate. Neil clearly had confidence in his tactical money management approach and knew the only way it would receive the attention it deserved was if Neil and Paul focused on it full time. Neil and Paul formed Good Harbor Financial.

One of the first actions taken by Neil and Paul was to recognize that CDOs trading at 5 cents on the dollar were way too cheap. Neil's valuation model was screaming buy, buy, buy. Neil and Paul put together a small fund and bought five CDO bonds backed by corporate debt rather than the more common mortgage debt. A year later, they sold one of the bonds and paid back all their investors. On the remaining four bonds, they nearly quintupled their money.

In 2009, Neil and Paul had figured out that the best way to market Neil's investment approach was through separately managed accounts sold through investment advisors. This was a market Neil and Paul knew virtually nothing about. Through a friend of a friend, they were introduced to Marcus Franklin. Three days later, Marcus was in charge of marketing.

Marcus and his wife sold their city condo and bought a tiny house in the suburbs. They got rid of the car and cable. They squeezed their expenses down to $1,500 per month. Marcus had just joined a firm with virtually no money, no website, no voice message recording, and no distribution.

The first Good Harbor office was too small for Neil, Paul, and Marcus to sit down at the same time. Being the third man in, Marcus had to figure out a solution. He went to the hardware store and bought basic home improvement supplies and built himself an office in the basement. He put the drywall up, installed the wiring, and hooked up the computer. He then literally duck taped the phone to his hand and started cold calling for 12 to 14 hours per day.

The investment management seed Neil had planted while at Motorola by taking active control of his 401(k) plan has become a powerful, prize-winning bull. Neil's strategy of staying out of major down markets is now called U.S. Tactical Core. The fund's 10-year anniversary was in April 2013. In a U.S. equity market that has experienced steady outflows since 2008, Neil's investment strategy has been pulling in hundreds of millions per month. In 2008, when the S&P 500 dropped by 37 percent, Neil's tactical strategy was down 0.07 percent, net of the management fee. With about the same level of volatility as the overall market, Neil's team has produced more than double the average annual returns of the S&P 500 with less than half of the maximum drawdown during their first 10 years.

Neil and the Good Harbor Financial management team measure risk perceptions. When investors demand a high risk premium to own equities, Good Harbor transitions 100 percent out of equities and into U.S. Treasuries. When risk levels are reduced and investors are more risk-seeking, Good Harbor buys broad equity market exposure through index ETFs. Rather than using a moving average crossover model to measure risk as we discussed in Chapter 7, Good Harbor monitors economic conditions, yield curve dynamics, and momentum measures in a disciplined, quantitative manner to make a monthly allocation decision. Fundamentally, Neil's quantitative risk premium model accomplishes the same objective as the moving average crossover model. They are winning by not losing. They are getting out of risk assets when risk levels are elevated. They are enjoying bullish equity market cycles when risk levels are attractive.

Back on the farm, Neil's mother and father were doing a bit of their own unconventional thinking. After spending years removing rocks from fields to grow hay for dairy cows, they began to take another look at the rocks. Maybe the rocks were the source of the farm's real value and not the cows or milk. It turned out that the farm was situated on a great vein perfect for commercial gravel extraction. Much like the youngest Peplinski finding his wealth by taking a fresh look at the investment landscape, Mr. and Mrs. Peplinski were finding their fortune by thinking about their farm in an entirely new way. Their fortune had been sitting directly in front of them for years.

When people ask Neil how he knows if his system will continue to work, he usually says the responsible thing: past results do not guarantee future returns. However, the idea that people's tolerance for risk changes as circumstances change is part of human nature. For the time-varying risk premium–based approach to stock investing to stop working, human nature and our feelings about fear and greed will have to change. We all want to make money in stocks and avoid major down markets. Many of us have been led to believe this is not possible. Much like the Peplinskis taking a fresh look at their farm from the standpoint of the rocks, Neil took a fresh look at the stock market and how it can be predictable on the basis of investors' variable tolerance for risk. Sometimes what is most obvious is hardest to see.

Neil, Paul, and Marcus work in the realm of ideas. They still get goose bumps as they watch how people go through a transforming experience as they get to know the Good Harbor tactical approach. The results of the strategy bring people to Good Harbor. When they come, they have a conversation. At the end of the conversation, people will often say, "That's the way I thought it always worked, but I was told I was wrong."

Many individual investors were hard hit by the 2000–2003 and 2007–2009 bear markets. All they had were a variety of buzzwords about MPT and diversification. Many investors are no longer willing to accept being told just to ride it out. Individuals are now asking their investment advisors what they are doing to protect their money. Most advisors do not have a good answer. They do not have a good systematic way to dynamically manage portfolios to avoid major down markets.

Peplinski's Takeaways

- Having seen the devastating effects of having an unhedged exposure to milk prices, Neil knew that a key element to risk management is limiting exposure during bearish market cycles. Neil's objective in looking at stock trading was to gain exposure in bullish cycles and limit exposure in bearish cycles.
- Being born with a mathematical mind and trained as an engineer, Neil preferred a systematic, nonemotional method to determine when markets are bullish or bearish. Neil wanted a model-based approach that could be back tested and then later used to compare actual results to model results to confirm the predictive power of the model.
- Neil determined that the best way to gain foresight on market movements was by evaluating investor perceptions of risk. Although measuring risk perceptions directly is difficult, Neil determined that there are many proxies for risk sentiment. When the proxies are measured and combined in a disciplined model, they are predictive of stock prices.

- Neil is focused on a primary and elemental driver of stock movement. He looks at tactical as being tactical with respect to market risk rather than allocating across different risky assets. Neil sees tactical as moving in and out of risk rather than shuffling positions among risky assets.

- Good Harbor's tactical approach was built by an engineer who was simply trying to optimize a way to stay out of major down markets in his 401(k) plan. Because he came from outside the finance area, his mind was not filled with finance theory. He had not been taught the "right" and "wrong" ways to think. Neil approached the problem with a completely open mind and a quest to find the truth. He was not looking to find data to prove or disprove any assertion or preexisting belief about investing. Rather, he looked for data that would lead to a more fundamental understanding of why stocks and the market move.

- Having an open mind and a desire to find the truth is an element shared by Sonny, Mr. M, Mike, and Neil. In many of these cases, money was being made in places and in a manner that the experts said was not possible. An open mind was a key to seeing a better path.

- Perhaps the most difficult aspect of taking advantage of market trends once you are able to recognize them and have a plan for how to act is having the discipline to stick with the plan. In Mike's case, the discipline was acquired through the painful lessons of the 1973–1974 bear market. In Neil's case, it comes from his strong analytical approach, in which his confidence in his ability to identify essential truths and linkages makes acting on these findings the only sensible course of action.

CHAPTER FIFTEEN

What Is Tactical Investing?

TACTICAL INVESTING is defined by Investopedia as "an active management portfolio strategy that rebalances the percentage of assets held in various categories in order to take advantage of market pricing anomalies or strong market sectors." Our definition of tactical investing is similar except that it emphasizes avoiding losses rather than trying to capture gains.

You should be a tactical equity investor if you believe the following:

1. There is a reasonable probability the stock market will experience a period of severe depreciation during your investment horizon. Such a loss and the time to get back to even would defeat your investment objectives.
2. There is a reasonable probability the stock market will not experience sufficient appreciation during your investment horizon to meet your investment objectives.
3. It makes sense to have a well-defined plan in place for addressing items 1 and 2 before you put money to work in equities.

Warren Buffett's first rule of investing is "don't lose money." His second rule of investing is "don't forget rule number one."

If we compare tactical investing to walking across a city street, our objective is to reach the other side safely, and the tactic we employ to accomplish this objective is to cross when there are no cars. We start the process by focusing on the possible downside of being struck and injured or killed rather than on the upside of getting to the other side of the street. Getting to the other side is not of interest if there is a high probability of being hit by a car. We do not enter the roadway until we have looked both ways to ensure that the chances of a negative event are as low as possible. By focusing on avoiding a major loss, we win.

The same thing is true with investing. Our objective is to increase our wealth by owning stocks. However, we have no interest in owning stocks if there is a reasonable chance that we will lose a significant portion of our wealth. Before entering the market, we look both ways to ensure that risk levels are attractive. If risk is unacceptably high, we stay out of the market. When risk is low, we proceed to invest.

Tactical investing is not new, though the way we are talking about it is.

John Maynard Keynes might be the first, best-known trader to use short-term indicators to predict the market. Keynes began his trading career in August 1919 at the age of 36. His broker offered him 10:1 leverage right out of the gate.

As an economist, he was bullish on the U.S. dollar and bearish on European currencies. He put his levered portfolio to work going long dollars and short the French franc, Italian lira, Indian rupee, German mark, and Dutch florin. By the spring of 1920, Keynes had more than quadrupled his initial equity and had begun to spend his paper gains without securing his wins by selling.

Like many forecasts involving complex systems, Keynes's currency projections proved less accurate as time extended. By May 1920, European currencies began to rally against the dollar. With 10:1 leverage and not having locked in his profits, Keynes was quickly wiped out. By the end of May, he received margin calls from his broker that would have put him into bankruptcy if it were not for loans from friends and the proceeds of his recently published book *The Economic Consequences of the Peace*. Keynes was able to scrape together the money he needed to continue trading. He had learned a valuable but painful lesson that led him to famously remark: "The market can stay irrational longer than you can stay solvent."

Having felt the bite of the market firsthand, Keynes became substantially less academic and theoretical, replacing sweeping economic forecasts with shorter-term trading indicators. By December 1920, he was able to pay back his lenders. Over the next four years, he had a return of 1,345 percent on his original equity amount. Prudently, he closed out those positions and was able to achieve financial independence.

One of the interesting lessons of Keynes's trading history is the fallacy of relying too much on long-term forecasts. Predicting anything very far into the future is difficult, even for the industry experts. Tom Watson, the founder of IBM, said, "I think there is a world market for maybe five computers." Ken Olsen, the founder of Digital Equipment, said, "There is no reason for any individual to have a computer in his home." On October 6, 1997, when asked if he were Steve Jobs, what would he do with Apple, Michael Dell said, "What would I do? I'd shut it down and give the money back to the shareholders." And on March 28, 2007, Federal Reserve Chairman Ben Bernanke, speaking in front of Congress, said that "the impact on the broader economy and financial markets of the problems in the subprime markets seems likely to be contained." Over the next two years, problems originating in the subprime mortgage market nearly caused a complete seizure of the U.S. economy. The United States was fully immersed in the Great Recession. Looking backward, it is hard to believe these intelligent experts got it so wrong.

One of the reasons statisticians do a poor job of predicting rare events is that they become overconfident as they gain more data. Confidence in the results of statistical calculations rises in a nonlinear manner as the sample size increases. Think of a political poll that involves 3 people versus a poll of 3,000. As the sample size increases, confidence that the projected result is accurate rises from virtually statistically irrelevant to a high 90 percent confidence level.

There are two problems with this. The first is that the fact that something is not represented in our sample size does not conclusively mean it does not exist. If you looked at market returns only from 1982 to 2000, you might have high confidence that the stock market appreciates at a low-teens rate. In fact, in 2000, many investors began to believe that this was the case. In short order, the Nasdaq dropped by more than 80 percent. The fact that we did not see a market down 80 percent from 1982 to 2000 does not mean that such events cannot exist.

The subprime mortgage market collapse that began in late 2007 was an example of an event that was unlikely to have been revealed by examination of a reasonably sized data set. In some sense, having an expert make the prediction may create a problem with the expert's having knowledge of a data set (built from his or her personal experience) that does not include the full range of possible outcomes. There expertness becomes a dangerous bias.

The other difficulty with forecasting by using probabilistic models is that probabilities are often not independent. Statistical math has made many intelligent people overestimate the precision of expected results (think LTCM). It is quite possible, in fact, that the probabilistic models often used in economics do not work well in the real world and have played an important role in misguiding investors on how to invest.

Because long-term predictions are so often wrong, tactical investing should involve using a systematic, disciplined model to make asset allocation decisions during a time frame when the chances of being right are high. Evaluations of market risk levels tend to be most accurate over a week to a month. Extending much farther greatly increases the level of uncertainty regarding the market view. Not only does looking too far out create forecasting problems, using too short a time frame also is problematic. Looking at a market by the hour or day often hides important intermediate-term trends with random volatility.

In making effective tactical market allocation decisions, there is a balance between being nimble and being whipsawed. Excessive trading may raise portfolio management expense and could detract from performance. Being too slow to move could expose the portfolio to a greater risk of experiencing a major setback.

When making a change to the portfolio asset allocation, do not move incrementally. Making partial changes to fund allocation is a way portfolio managers hedge against being completely wrong. Rather than place all of their investment in one area, they invest in all areas. Investing in all areas is a way to virtually guarantee that the portfolio will be exposed to loss and negates the purpose of active management. If your tactical model works, be disciplined and act on it.

One major problem with some tactical investment methods is that they do too little to make a difference. Think of your typical long-only equity mutual fund altering its cash holds from 2 percent to 12 percent of the total fund value. In a major down market, this small adjustment will not make much of a difference as measured by absolute performance.

After the 2008–2009 stock market collapse, many of the major mutual fund institutions brought to market tactical mutual funds. Many of these funds have shown poor results. The primary reason for this is that most of the funds move incrementally. When they are bearish on the stock market, they continue to have exposure. When they are bullish, they tend not to increase exposure sufficiently to take advantage of the uptrend.

Maybe most important, equity mutual funds have generally maintained high equity exposures for the last three or four decades. Moving funds in and out of risk assets (stocks) is not what they do. Their investment processes and marketing focus are all about buying stocks, not selling them. Virtually none of these institutions spent any time developing tactical investment models over the last 10 or 20 years. They are making a cold start in a difficult area where they have little institutional commitment.

It is critical when selecting a tactical asset manager that you find one who has a long-term, real-money, audited track record of success in this style of investing. Many firms are marketing new tactical funds on the basis of back tested results. We suspect you will never see any firm market poor back tested results. Often, firms will back test several strategies and see which one produces the best results looking backward. This style of strategy selection has a high probability of producing poor results going forward. Market cycles change, and the fact that a model works on a back tested basis for a segment of market history does little to assure that it will work during all cycles. As a final word of caution regarding back tested results, real-world trading frictions (time of day trades are executed, miscellaneous execution problems, fees, etc.) almost always skew to the downside the conversion of back tested results to true audited results.

At a minimum, the track record should extend back at least to 2007 to evaluate fund performance during the credit crisis. The 2008 meltdown distorted securities markets and humiliated the world's shrewdest money managers. Diversification strategies failed, and many mutual fund owners and individuals with privately managed accounts incurred losses near 50 percent. The average hedge fund was down 21 percent in 2008. The bottom 10 percent of funds plummeted by nearly twice the market's decline: 62.4 percent. Others evaporated entirely. A surprising number of the smartest guys in the room became illiquid.

Tactical investing, even successful tactical investing, has costs. The three primary costs of tactical investing are as follows:

1. *The price of short-term trading.* Although trading costs have declined over the years, trading usually is associated with commission costs. Lots of short-term trades can create a performance drag, all else being equal. More important than commission costs are the tax consequences of short-term trading. The difference between long-term capital gain tax rates and ordinary income tax rates is substantial currently.
2. *The price of whipsaws.* The risk of being whipsawed generally entails buying and selling the market while the market is in a trendless state. These trading moves usually do not provide positive performance and cause a portfolio to experience higher short-term trading costs.
3. *Missing the important up moves.* Although missing the 10 biggest up days in the market is less important than missing the 10 worst days from a portfolio return standpoint, the risk of being out of the market during a major rally is part of market timing. If the

tactical strategy has a record of avoiding major down markets, the risk of missing the up markets is greatly minimized as it is no longer the essential element that will drive a portfolio's expected return.

Because avoidance of major down markets carries priority over trading tax efficiency, tactical asset management works best in a tax-deferred account such as an IRA. In these types of accounts, trading gains are not taxed on an annual basis. Generally, no taxes are paid until money is withdrawn. The expectation is that the individual's tax rate will be low during the withdrawal period as the person is often retired. In some cases, tactical investment programs have such strong performance that even when held in a taxable account, they continue to show material outperformance of the broad stock market benchmarks.

Tactical Takeaways

- Focus on avoiding major losses rather than chasing gains.
- Make decisions that are based on a time frame in which the chances of being right are maximized.
- Do not move incrementally. Being partially hit by a car is not much different from being hit by a car. Get completely out of the way.
- Use a repeatable, systematic, and disciplined method for making tactical decisions. Making major asset allocation decisions is difficult to do consistently and profitably if your emotions are in control.
- If possible, hold your tactical investments in tax-deferred accounts.

To buy and hold stocks and not have a systematic, disciplined plan for avoiding major loss is like buying a home or car and not having an insurance policy. Insurance policies are not perfect, but they go a long way toward mitigating loss when the house burns down or the crash occurs.

CHAPTER SIXTEEN

The Story of Vinay Munikoti

W E HAVE met a lot of traders over the years who have developed systems to outperform the market with less risk. Many of these traders have failed to fully account for asymmetric risk or all the risk to which their systems are exposed. Their trading systems break down as the underlying behavior of the stock market changes over time. What makes the traders we discuss in this book stand out is their appreciation of risk and the way they manage risk. As a result, their outperformance has stood the test of time. What makes Vinay Munikoti stand out even more is his understanding of how the changing risk premium in the equity market can be favorably traded in the bond market.

Vinay Munikoti was born in Lausanne, Switzerland, on the shores of Lake Geneva. His father was finishing up some academic work in physics at a Swiss university after earning his PhD. Four years later, the family moved to New Brunswick, Canada. Shortly afterward, they moved to Bangalore, India. Within a few years, they were on the move again and this time ended up in Ottawa, Canada. Having traveled the world before reaching college age, Vinay was at ease letting the flow of life take him wherever it might.

In college in Ottawa, Vinay studied mechanical engineering. Hockey, snowshoes, and canoes never really got him excited. What Vinay enjoyed most was quantitative modeling and analysis. He was on the cusp of taking a circuitous journey into the world of financial engineering and quantitative analysis, where he would seek to push forward the boundaries of finance.

Upon graduating from college, Vinay secured an engineering job with a Canadian-based telecommunications company in San Jose, California. One day while driving to work, he heard a radio advertisement for a get-rich-quick scheme involving trading options on heating oil futures. The complexity of trading options on futures fascinated Vinay, and so he picked up the phone and called the broker in Florida. The broker promised quick and sure-thing profits based on projections of a colder than expected winter. Vinay, more fascinated with the interplay of complex derivatives securities than with the possibility of making money, pushed aside thoughts about the bloated commissions and began to trade.

Although the make-huge-profits-now scheme for trading heating oil turned out to be a way to pay a broker high commissions, Vinay's life course had been permanently altered. Within a year of sitting in a cubicle developing engineering solutions for his employer, Vinay could not rid himself of his fascination for the far more quantitative and complex world of financial engineering.

He quit his job, moved to New York, and enrolled in a technical institute to take master's-level classes in financial engineering, including portfolio theory, options theory, and risk management, at night. By day, Vinay found employment validating interest rate derivative pricing models, analyzing systematic equity strategies, and performing other miscellaneous high-level quant analyst work. After finishing his master's degree, he spent the next several years working at quantitative money management firms, designing and refining computer code for momentum trading systems and developing portfolio/risk systems.

In 2005, Vinay received a call from an old colleague. The colleague was in the process of raising money for a commodities futures trend-following product in the alternative investment space and needed a creative quant guy to do the programming. Vinay agreed to join the venture, and they began operations with $20 million of seed capital from an insurance company.

In the world of institutional quantitative finance, the smallest things can trip you up. In Vinay's case, the problem was that their trading strategy had a correlation of 70 to 80 percent with the peer group, which created a problem raising money. If this sounds like reverse Chinese to you, that is okay. Although conceptually the world of quantitative finance is relatively simple, its effective implementation and the metrics it is measured by are challenging and complex. Gross returns from a strategy may be attractive, but if a myriad of other performance metrics do not measure up, institutions will not invest. Everything institutional investors do has to be explained to boards of directors, and lengthy performance reporting is the language spoken to justify positions. In any event, Vinay knew this venture would face headwinds in raising new assets. With this realization, he quit.

Shortly after he left his job, Lehman Brothers collapsed. Wall Street was in free fall. Jobs vanished. In Vinay's case, he did not feel much anxiety. He had been raised to roam and was comfortable with the uncertainty of constant motion. Vinay was not on Wall Street solely to make money. He was there to immerse himself in complex quantitative modeling, where he could explain the real world with math. He enjoyed building predictive models by using a multitude of factors to create a stable, systematic way to profitably trade.

In the analytical world of finance, lots of technicians are really good at reporting on various sources of risk. Many of them are mathematically strong but lack creativity or the spark to do something really good in a creative way. They do what their bosses want and try not to push boundaries. Vinay was on a different path. His quest was to build the perfect trading model, one that had a high Sharpe ratio and was not correlated with other trading strategies.

While building and maintaining the commodity futures trading program used to trade insurance company money, he never stopped thinking about and working on his objective of building a more robust quant model. Textbook portfolio theory was of little use to Vinay except for general concepts such as the idea of dampening volatility through diversification. He also knew from experience that dynamically evolving portfolio-weighting tools based on trailing covariance are generally not stable and do not work well in the real world. He was pushing the boundaries of finance forward. He was working on novel ways of creating diversification within single-asset strategies by combining information about the price action of an instrument with macro drivers operating under the surface.

In late 2008, he was ready to show the world his work. He had created a systematic way to evaluate macro and momentum indicators in a simple output expressed through the 30-year U.S. Treasury bond. He met with an insurance firm in the Northwest that allocated $17 million to his strategy. Today he is managing hundreds of millions.

Delta Investment Management currently offers a long-term Treasury bond trading strategy reflective of Vinay's work. It has been proved to be an important money maker and overall risk management device because of its inverse correlation to bearish equity markets while having positive correlation with bullish equity markets. In 2008, the strategy delivered almost a 60 percent return versus the S&P 500 declining by 37 percent including dividends.

Munikoti Takeaways

What is common to Sonny, Mike, Neil, and Vinay is their quest for a disciplined, systematic way to control risk and be appropriately positioned for risk-on/risk-off market environments. Controlling risk boils down to avoiding significant losses. Participating in up markets involves identifying and investing in a positive trend.

One interesting facet of Vinay's quantitative trading system is the use of long-term Treasuries rather than equities. Vinay's trading models evaluate changing risk perceptions. When investors become interested in a return of their principal rather than a return on their principal, they tend to run to secure investments such as U.S. Treasuries. Increased demand for Treasuries places downward pressure on interest rates. Not only does increased demand lower yields, but the Federal Reserve often acts to lower interest rates during times of economic stress.

When interest rates decline, bond prices rise. The longer the duration of the bond, the more dramatic the bond price movement in relation to interest rate changes.

In 2008, many investors asked us why our tactical programs did not short the market when the indicators were bearish. If investors had shorted the S&P 500 in 2008, they could have achieved a 37 percent gain. However, had they been long the 30-year Treasury through Vinay's tactical program, they would have been up roughly 60 percent. Owning 30-year Treasuries can be considered less "risky" on a number of metrics relative to shorting.

What Vinay discovered is a way to trade changes in investor risk tolerance by using an instrument that simplifies the trading process and provides potentially excellent positive returns in down markets. Conversely, Vinay's tactical strategy also can excel during rising interest rate environments. When investors are becoming more risk-seeking and interest rates are on the rise, Vinay's system can benefit by being long an inverse 30-year U.S. Treasury instrument.

PART TWO

Applying a Tactical Trading Discipline to Profit from Investable Equity Market Trends

CHAPTER SEVENTEEN

Capturing the Ups and Missing the Downs: Five Steps

S O FAR, you have read stories about people who were able to profit during winning periods and avoid major losing periods by reducing their investment exposure. We have listed general takeaways, academic considerations, and real-world observations that should be considered when you are investing.

We now switch gears and offer applied and specific methods for participating in bullish markets and avoiding major bearish markets. These easy-to-follow investment tactics have proved successful in protecting wealth in major equity bear markets and building wealth through participation in major equity bull markets.

Right up front we want to make it clear that we are not talking about day trading. Over very short periods ranging from seconds to days, market fluctuations will essentially be random measured against our ability to predict them. Over intermediate-term periods, we are able to predict aggregate price levels with a high degree of success.

Step 1: When to Buy and Sell: Learn to Identify Bullish and Bearish Markets

Have you ever heard the saying "It's a stock picker's market"? Usually, when you hear that phrase, someone is trying to tell you that a selection of carefully screened stocks will outperform the benchmark index. Although this could be true from time to time, it somewhat misses the point. The real question should be: "Should you pick

BARRON'S

As of: 04/04/2013 15:17:16 ET

Delta Tactical Market Sentiment

The Delta MSI measures the position of ~3,600 stocks relative to an intermediate-term moving average crossover (MAC) point. When greater than 50% of the stocks followed are above this MAC point, the market is bullish and equities are attractive. When the indicator is below 50%, risk is elevated and stock exposures should be reduced. Manager uses discretion on asset allocation when MSI is 50% +/- 3%.

CURRENT SENTIMENT	LAST WEEK	2 WEEKS AGO	3 WEEKS AGO
BULLISH	67.1%	72.6%	76.5%

Current Market Exposure: 100% Equities, 0% Cash
Source: Delta Investment Management
www.deltaim.com, (415) 249-6337

the market?" In other words, if the stock market is showing strong appreciation, it is likely you could randomly select any basket of about 20 stocks and do about as well as, if not better than, the overall market. Conversely, if the market is in a bear move, you will be hard pressed to find a basket of stocks that consistently makes you a lot of money. The important question is whether you should be in the market at all.

Over the years, we have seen all types of trading strategies deployed to earn superior returns. These strategies include mean-reversion/contrarian strategies; information pricing lag arbitrage; growth stock buying based on price/earnings (P/E) ratios and price/earnings to growth (PEG) ratios; value stock buying based on book value, cash flow, and/or break-up value; the calendar effect (holiday, weekend, end of quarter, etc.); and seasonal trades, among others. We have seen the most sophisticated short selling technologies and hedging strategies. We have actively engaged in cross-asset class arbitrage, in which price action in one asset class with better-informed participants (e.g., institutional options trading, credit default swaps, insider buying/selling patterns) is useful for predicting pricing in the stock market.

But all these strategies fail to ask a basic question: Do you want to be trading stocks at all? We know that when the market is under the influence of strong selling pressure, it does not matter which stocks you own because the majority are headed south. As the selling pressure intensifies, so does the wanton selling of any asset at any price. The mark of a major bear market is that eventually everything in your portfolio loses money.

Our recommendation is to enter the stock market when the perceived market risk is moderate and declining. We make no effort to buy at the bottom. The reason we are not attempting to buy the market bottom is that bottoms may be false (the risk of "catching the falling knife") and markets often show maximum volatility when they are under the greatest amount of risk premium stress. We are focused on capturing a significant portion of the upward trend. We would rather see a market begin to recover before committing capital. Conversely, we are not particularly concerned with selling at the market apex. We seek to predict when market pricing is likely to deteriorate on the basis of changes in the aggregate risk premium. We are asking ourselves constantly if the expected risk/reward in the market warrants an investment in equities.

We attempt to invest in stocks when the chances of losing money are minimal. We seek to avoid the stock market when the chances of making money are minimal. For the market in the aggregate, stocks generally rise when perceived risk is falling and fall when perceived risk is rising. To know when to be in and out of the stock market, we have to be able to measure investors' risk perceptions.

Note that we are not talking about being in and out of the market on the basis of valuation. Knowing that the average P/E on the S&P 500 for the last 20 years has been roughly 15 and the current P/E is 12, for example, is hardly predictive of future stock prices over the intermediate term.

What is predictive is investor perceptions about how certain the earnings are and in which direction they are headed. Investors' perceptions about the certainty of earnings are wrapped up in their feelings about whether they see the world as risky or safe. A perception of increasing risks has a high correlation with declining P/E multiples and equity values. If investors collectively see risk as moderating,

P/Es and equities rise. Much of the time, actual printed earnings forecasts do not change much.

To measure risk, quantitative traders monitor economic output and consumption and growth rates, corporate credit spreads, volatility measures, momentum indicators, and yield curve dynamics. Although all these inputs are highly informative if you have developed a robust, quantitative system for compiling them and producing an output that accurately predicts whether equity risk premiums are rising or falling, we suspect you do not have such a model and are not about to develop one.

The good news is that extensive research and actual fund performance show that a simple moving average crossover (MAC) model to determine when the market is bullish or bearish is as effective in improving investment returns as are these more elaborate multifactor models. A moving average crossover system can provide a simple means of letting you know when to be invested in stocks and when to sell your stocks and position your portfolio defensively. Efficient or partially efficient markets show a great deal of information about investor sentiment through pricing. Rising prices are one of the best, if not the best, indicators that investor risk premiums are declining. The same is true for falling prices and rising risk premiums.

In 2009, Theodore Wong, a graduate of the Massachusetts Institute of Technology (MIT) with BSEE and MSEE degrees, combined his engineering analytics and econometrics modeling skills to study risk management in both up and down markets. What he discovered is that an investor who bought the market when the market broke above its six-month moving average and sold the market when it traded below it far outperformed a buy-and-hold investor.

The following are several selections from the study performed by Theodore Wong titled "Moving Average: Holy Grail or Fairy Tale" published by Advisor Perspectives in June 2009.

- "Buying and holding a diversified portfolio works well during good times, but falls short when supposedly uncorrelated assets classes drop in unison in bear markets."

- "The moving average crossover (MAC) is the simplest and probably the oldest trading system. You buy when the price rises above its moving average, and you sell when it drops below."
- "Based on aggregate performance over the entire 138-year period, the MAC system beats buy-and-hold in both absolute performance and risk-adjusted return."

Figure 17.1 shows the study results for the six-month moving average versus the S&P 500.

Mr. Wong concludes: "There is no fairy tale if a system can consistently avoid the losers but stay with the winners 1,659 times over 138 years." Academic studies can be thought-provoking but also difficult to replicate in the real world. In evaluating any stock trading

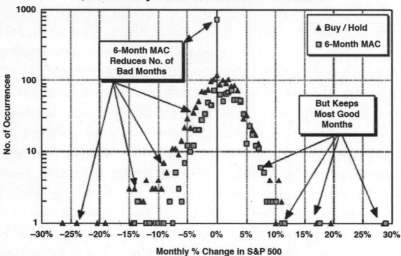

FIGURE 17.1 Six-Month MAC Model Avoids Major Down Markets and Produces Higher CAGR Than Does Buy and Hold

Source: *Advisor Perspectives*, "Moving Average: Holy Grail or Fairy Tale, Part 2," by Theodore Wong, June 30, 2009.

advice, you should ask if the system is based on an audited record of real-money trades over a long period.

Howard Hebert started publishing market timing signals in the early 1970s. His signals are primarily tied to intermediate- and longer-term moving average crossover models. Hebert has recorded his market timing signals since December 17, 1971. With these signals, his timing produced a 13 percent average annual rate of return versus the S&P 500 return of 9.5 percent through July 25, 2012; in this case, $10,000 invested at a 13 percent annual return grows to $1,327,816 over 40 years, whereas $10,000 invested at a 9.5 percent annual return grows to $377,194. Market timing using Hebert's MAC system improved investment results by a factor of 3.5× over this time frame.

Delta Investment Management, as part of its money management services, monitors the 75-day simple moving average on a group of roughly 3,600 stocks to determine bullish and bearish market phases. When the majority of stocks in the market are trading above their 75-day moving average, the market is bullish. When the majority of stocks are trading under this level, the market is bearish. A reliable and accurate way to make a bullish/bearish market determination is to visit our website at www.deltaim.com and sign up for our free weekly Market Sentiment Indicator (MSI) report. If you would like a full report e-mailed to you for free every Friday, let us know by contacting us at www.deltaim.com.

The Delta Investment Management Market Sentiment Indicator is also published in *Barron's* every week and can be found online on the *Barron's* website. In print, it appears in the Market Laboratory Indicators section of the paper under the heading "Delta Market Sentiment Indicator." Both *Barron's* and the weekly report sent by e-mail from the www.deltaim.com website show the indicator value and its trend.

The two parts of Figure 17.2 show what the market bullish/bearish signals would be if you simply applied a 75-day moving average to the S&P 500 since the start of 2008. It is evident that this elemental way

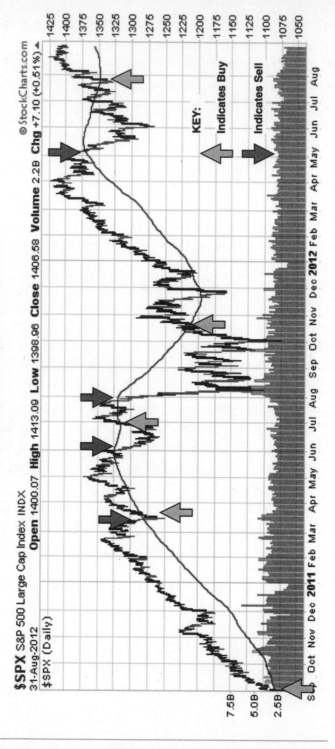

75-Day MAC Buy/Sell Signals
vs.
S&P 500 (SPX)
September 2010–September 2012

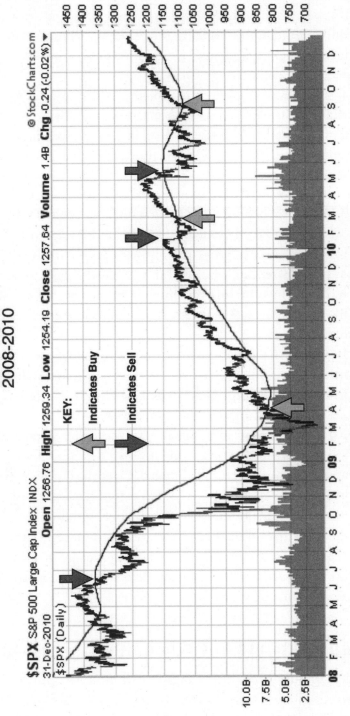

FIGURE 17.2 Seventy-Five-Day MAC Buy/Sell Signals Applied to the S&P 500, 2008–2010 and September 2010–October 2012

of avoiding major down markets has a tremendous positive impact on portfolio returns. Additionally, the 75-day moving average does not trigger excessive trading and a disproportionate run-up in portfolio management costs.

Investors who employed a disciplined, nonemotional 75-day MAC method for investing in bullish markets and exiting bearish markets made money in the 1970s secular bear market and during the nontrending market period from 2000 through 2012. Consider the following:

- The premise behind identifying bullish and bearish market phases is based on evaluating investors' risk tolerance. If investors are increasingly risk-seeking, equities are likely to rise as stock buyers are willing to accept a lower expected rate of return. If investors are becoming more risk-averse, stocks are likely to depreciate as investors demand a higher expected rate of return.
- Investor risk perceptions are far more volatile than formal institutional sell-side analyst consensus estimates. Changes in investor risk perceptions explain a significant portion of stock movement in the short and intermediate term.
- Risk perceptions can be measured. One of the oldest and most reliable methods of measuring investor risk perceptions is to use a moving average crossover model. Over the last 40 years, the 75-day simple moving average has demonstrated strong results.
- Some of the major drawbacks associated with market timing are missing times of market appreciation and incurring the extra expense of trading. The 75-day moving average is sufficiently nimble to avoid major down markets without being so nimble as to create excessive trading costs.

Step 2: What to Buy When the Market Is Bullish

When you use a moving average crossover model, you have a basic tool by which to judge market risk and predict bullish and bearish cycles. However, knowing the market is bullish or bearish solves only a portion of the problem. The remaining challenge is knowing what to buy during bullish and bearish phases. In Step 2, we address the question of what to buy when the market signal is bullish.

Paul Samuelson once said, "Bombarding yourself with lots of plausible [stock] stories is guaranteed to accelerate the turnover of your portfolio and help pay for your broker's yacht. As true today, in the twenty-first century, as it was in the mid-twentieth century." What Samuelson was talking about is the ability of the stocks of many businesses to seem like compelling buys. There are companies working on curing cancer. Some companies are working on next-generation energy systems, including fuel cells and nuclear fusion reactors. Apple (AAPL) has a long history of producing products that consumers can't wait to own.

The reality is that no matter how attractive an investment case may sound, picking winning stocks on the basis of their stories is difficult. In evaluating stocks, it is often far more productive to ignore stories and focus on price signals. High relative strength stocks are stocks which are showing the strongest price appreciation over a period of time. This group of stocks has tended to deliver superior returns relative to the broad market.

William O'Neil is a believer in high relative strength stocks. In 1984, O'Neil began to publish his database ranking stocks by relative strength in a publication called *Investor's Business Daily* (IBD). Today, at www.investors.com, the online version of *Investor's Business Daily*, O'Neil maintains an index called the IBD 85–85. This index represents a group of stocks that are in the top 15 percent of the market as measured by relative strength and earnings strength. IBD's research shows that in every market over the last 50 years, the best performing stocks have had EPS and relative strength ratings of 85 percent or higher before they made their biggest gains.

Figure 17.3 is a chart of the IBD 85–85 Index versus the S&P 500 from November 13, 2000, to December 31, 2012.

In this figure, buy-and-hold investors in the S&P 500 during the time frame shown experienced a cumulative return of about

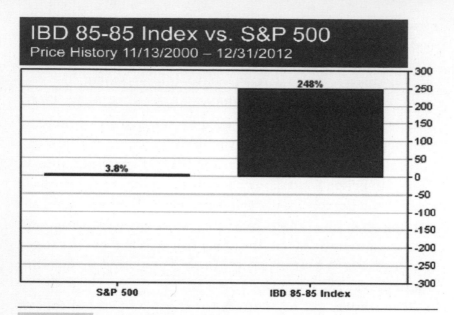

FIGURE 17.3 High Relative Strength Stocks versus the S&P 500

Source: Investors.com; *Investor's Business Daily.*

3.8 percent. Investors who maintained a portfolio that mimicked the IBD 85–85 Index had a return that was roughly 248 percent over the same period. None of this outperformance was the result of having reduced equity exposure to less than 100 percent. In other words, even with the 2000–2003 Nasdaq stock meltdown and the 2008–2009 credit crisis bear market, high relative strength stocks outperformed the broad market by a tremendous amount. Imagine how much better the returns could have been if in addition to owning high relative strength stocks, an investor also missed the major market sell-offs by using a MAC model to guide asset allocation trade decisions.

Dorsey, Wright & Associates is also an expert on high relative strength stocks. In January 2010, Dorsey, Wright & Associates published its "real-world" testing of relative strength study results. Figure 17.4 is a summary table of those results. In 100 percent of the trials, high relative strength stocks outperformed the market, with an average return of 227.1 percent versus the S&P 500 return of 81.0 percent.

Table 1: Summary Data (Cumulative Returns) 12/29/95—12/31/09	
# of Trials	100
Average Return	227.1%
Median Return	214.8%
Max Return	446.4%
Top Quartile	263.4%
Bottom Quartile	181.0%
Min Return	94.2%
S&P 500 Return	81.0%
% Trials Outperform	100%

FIGURE 17.4 Dorsey, Wright & Associates High Relative Strength Stock Return Study Results

Source: Dorsey, Wright & Associates.

If you buy a portfolio of high relative strength stocks, we recommend that you maintain a diversified portfolio. Each position should be initiated with an equal weighting, and the portfolio should include at least 20 stocks. Stocks purchased for the portfolio should have a relative strength measurement in the top quintile.

Another successful tactic during bullish market cycles is to build a portfolio that has broad equity market exposure by using index equity ETFs or mutual funds. Modern finance theory mostly classifies risk as volatility. If you buy the market index, you should expect to see exactly the same amount of volatility in your portfolio that is experienced by the market. Market volatility is called beta. If on a periodic basis you transition 100 percent out of the market index and into asset classes with less than equity market volatility such as cash or bonds, you should expect to have lower portfolio volatility than the market index through the full investment cycle. Cash is generally assumed to have zero volatility, and bonds, depending on their duration, credit quality, and type, are usually less volatile than equities. When you average some amount of time with market volatility and less than market volatility, the average portfolio volatility is less than market volatility measured by itself.

We have already made the case that an investor can improve long-term expected returns by owning the market during bullish cycles and reducing equity exposure to zero during bearish cycles by using a simple 75-day moving average. As a result of transitioning from stocks to less volatile assets periodically, an investor should expect this style of management to reduce overall portfolio volatility. Not only does this portfolio outperform on an absolute basis, it has better risk-adjusted returns (lower volatility).

If the same investors were willing to accept portfolio volatility equal to the market, they could then increase their expected volatility during times they are invested in equities, as the higher in-the-market volatility would be offset by the lower out-of-the equity market volatility. These investors could raise the in-the-market portfolio beta to a level at which the average of in-the-market and out-of-the market volatility is equal to the market volatility on its own.

The reason an investor might actually seek to increase portfolio volatility to equal that of the overall stock market is as follows:

- Up and down volatility are not the same. Up volatility is good, and most investors seek better than market performance in bullish cycles.
- Using the MAC model, the investor owns stocks during bullish market cycles when the overall stock market is expected to appreciate. By increasing volatility (beta) during bullish cycles, the investor should expect to outperform the market by the amount of excess beta greater than 1. Increasing beta during bullish cycles improves what is known as upside market capture.
- Using the MAC model, the investor will transition 100 percent out of stocks and into some other, less volatile defensive asset class during bearish cycles. As a result, the investor's portfolio should show much less than market volatility during bearish events.
- In using a MAC model to manage your portfolio, increasing overall portfolio volatility to equal that of the broad stock market is all about seeking to outperform in both up and down

markets. The objective is to have a portfolio that acts like a stock in up markets and participates fully in bullish moves and acts like cash or bonds in a down market and sidesteps the bearish equity moves. The investor is building a non–hedge fund hedge fund, in other words, an equitylike fund with strong downside protection, full transparency, immediate liquidity, low fees, and incredible risk-adjusted returns.

When invested in equities, we often use a portfolio that has greater than market beta. In an up market, for example, a portfolio with a beta of 1.3 should have an expected return 30 percent greater than that of the market. Again, when the market is in a bearish phase, the portfolio transitions to assets with low or zero beta (U.S. Treasuries and cash), bringing down the overall average beta of the portfolio measured over time to be equivalent to the market beta of 1. Portfolio beta should be adjusted over time to keep abreast of current market conditions and investor risk tolerance.

Although the discussion of beta may seem complex, there are some very easy ways to own a market portfolio with a beta different from that of the S&P 500. You can blend levered and unlevered ETFs or mutual funds in your portfolio in a ratio that matches your desired portfolio beta target. Additionally, some broad market ETFs and mutual funds have betas greater than the S&P 500. When constructing your bull market equity portfolio, keep an eye on beta.

In Step 2, the fundamental idea is to be aggressive when participating in up markets. During bullish market cycles, it is rare to see anyone lose a lot of money. Risk levels are attractive, and investors should take full advantage of the opportunity. High relative strength stocks have a strong track record of delivering outperformance, especially during bullish market cycles. If you prefer to gain market exposure by using broad market index ETFs or mutual funds, consider increasing portfolio beta. This will create excellent upside market capture, and because you have an investment plan that will reduce equity exposure in bearish market periods, you should experience a favorable up to down market capture ratio. If investing aggressively during bullish cycles creates anxiety, remember that you have a plan for avoiding major down markets.

Step 3: What to Own During Bearish Periods

The purpose of managing money tactically is to protect capital during bearish equity market cycles and participate in bullish market cycles. When markets turn bearish, the primary nonequity alternative investment vehicles are cash and bonds. An investor may also consider the possibility of shorting equities during bearish cycles. This third alternative has become easier with the introduction of inverse index ETFs and mutual funds.

The primary benefit of owning cash in a bearish market is obvious: no losses. Owning cash achieves the tactical objective of capital preservation during bearish market cycles. Cash has zero volatility and reduces overall portfolio volatility measured over time. Cash provides maximum liquidity during a time when many other investment vehicles become less liquid. During severely bearish markets, a 100 percent cash position provides maximum flexibility for investing opportunistically when prices are distressed.

Some tactical investors seek a return above that of cash when they are out of stocks. The safest source of yield is U.S. Treasuries. Unlike cash, there is a risk of price fluctuation with U.S. Treasuries. This risk is amplified the farther out on the maturity curve the investor extends. Thirty-year Treasury bond prices are generally more volatile than short duration (1 year or less) Treasury bills.

Figure 17.5 shows a chart of monthly returns for stocks and bonds during recessions (source of recession dates: NBER) from 1981 through 2008.

Two observations stand out. First, potential bond returns are material. The possibility of capturing 1.55 percent a month in a 10-year Treasury fund during an economic downturn is attractive. Second, on average bonds outperform stocks in both the front half and the back half of a recession. Bond outperformance in both halves of a recession means that the forecast regarding the business cycle does

Market Environment (1981-2008)	Average Monthly Return				
	Large Cap	Mid Cap	Small Cap	10-Yr Bond	5-Yr Bond
Recessions	−0.83%	−0.42%	−0.52%	1.55%	1.31%
Front Half of Recession	−1.56%	−1.04%	−2.08%	0.71%	0.82%
Back Half of Recession	0.03%	0.31%	1.32%	2.54%	1.88%

FIGURE 17.5 Stock and Bond Returns During Recessions

Source: Good Harbor Financial.

not need to be overly precise. Depending on how much volatility you are comfortable with in your portfolio, you can set the duration of your Treasury bond holdings anywhere from 1 to 30 years, with the long dated Treasuries being the most volatile.

Corporate bonds carry a higher yield than Treasury bonds but have much higher volatility. In very severe downturns such as the 2008–2009 credit crisis, corporate bonds act increasingly like stocks (correlations start to approach 1). As company earnings fall, stock prices decline. With earnings falling and credit markets becoming very tight, bond default risk rises. As corporate bonds trade more on default risk than on interest rate risk, they behave increasingly like equities. We do not view corporate bonds as a suitable investment vehicle for achieving capital protection during bearish cycles.

If tactical systems predict both bullish and bearish market cycles, an investor might wonder why he or she should not short sell equities during bearish cycles. The simple answer is that the primary objective of tactical investing is to achieve high risk-adjusted returns through active risk management. Risk management is achieved by limiting portfolio exposure to negative volatility. Shorting involves potentially high exposure to negative volatility.

In 2008, the U.S. government banned shorting stocks on a list of almost 1,000 heavily shorted equities. When the no-short list was issued, many investors lost a tremendous amount of money. In over-crowded shorts, there is always the risk of a short squeeze. A short squeeze (too many investors attempting to cover their short positions all at once) can cause rapid equity appreciation and loss of value in a portfolio. The average hedge fund was down over 21 percent in 2008. When you examine the detailed results of many hedge funds in all market cycles, rarely does the short side of their portfolios add to absolute performance. For us, the risk of shorting stocks is unacceptably high.

In major down markets, cash is the safest asset. Thus, for those looking for the most conservative vehicle, cash is king. If we protect capital in major down markets, there is a high probability that we will build wealth over time. For investors interested in enhancing returns during bearish cycles, U.S. Treasuries can be an effective safe haven that offers potential returns greater than zero.

Step 4: Take the Emotion Out of Your Investment Strategy

Students of investment behavior have long noted that people have a hard time letting go of losers. Status quo bias is the behavioral finance diagnosis for this error, and the reasoning goes like this: "If I don't sell, the stock might go back up and I will have been right all along. Even worse, if I do sell and then the stock goes up, I'll really feel dumb." This problem, by the way, is hardly limited to amateurs. It is why pension trustees insist that their money managers spell out a strict sell discipline.

Reluctance to sell is a difficult barrier to overcome. But once positions have been sold, it is almost harder to buy them back again if market signals indicate that this is the appropriate course of action. This is often referred to as cognitive dissonance. Most investors are uncomfortable acting in a manner that is 180 degrees the opposite of a recent previous action.

Emotions often cause investors to miss important bull cycles and remain exposed during bear cycles. Our emotions are often our worst enemy. In bullish markets, investor interest often occurs near market tops. When stocks depreciate, investors often become emotionally tied to their positions and justify holding on because the stocks are becoming so "cheap." At some point, many investors reach the "give up" moment and sell at the bottom.

Taking emotion out of investing is all about having an investment plan in advance of investing and being disciplined about implementing the plan. Sonny, Mr. M, Mike, Neil, and Vinay all approached their investment path with a detailed, systematic buy/sell plan and a strong discipline to execute on the plan. We know from our personal interactions with these investors that it is often emotionally difficult to stay on course and be loyal to one's method. Having the discipline to stay on plan and get out of the way of major down markets is the most important and most difficult element of tactical investing.

Having an investment plan does not require that an investor have some special ability to forecast economic conditions. Even if an investor had perfect knowledge of the economic climate five years from now, it is far from certain that that knowledge would lead to an obvious investment course. The world is a complex place, and rarely do events go directly from A to B in a straight line.

The successful tactical investment strategies we are discussing are not based on forecasting the long-term economic future. They rely on having a proven, systematic method for evaluating changing investor risk perceptions over the short and intermediate terms. Although broad economic forecasts and sweeping insights about where the economy is headed are of interest, they play almost no role in a disciplined, non-emotional tactical investment program.

One way to start the process of removing emotions from your investment process is to turn off the TV. The media are rough on investors; at any given time, they will present 10 reasons to buy and 10 reasons to sell. They focus on what is sensational rather than what might really matter. The emotional roller coaster fueled by the media can be a nightmare and is often counterproductive.

When one has a tactical plan and sticks with the discipline, the investment process migrates from the realm of emotions to the realm of calculated risk taking. With a plan for avoiding major losses in place, investors find the task of investing much less stressful.

Step 5: Start Today

If you have gotten this far in the book, you may be reaching a point where you are thinking more seriously about actively managing your portfolio by using a tactical approach. You still may have a couple of nagging concerns. The first is that your broker/investment advisor informed you that all studies of market timing show it does not work. The advisor may say it is ill advised to even attempt to time the market.

The simple response is that Mike, Good Harbor, Vinay, and others can show strong case histories of beating the market by using a tactical approach. The managers who run Yale's endowment made average annual returns of about 10 percent over the 10 years ending June 30, 2011. For 2012, they had a 6 percent U.S. equity buy-and-hold allocation and a 53 percent allocation in actively managed absolute return and private equity funds. Princeton's allocation to actively managed absolute return and private equity funds is 48 percent. Stanford's allocation is 30 percent, and Harvard's is 28 percent.

The same experts who tell you it is fruitless to attempt to time the market use stock and industry research reports that have a rating printed prominently on the front cover. The recommendation often says "buy," "hold," or "sell." Is this not a market timing recommendation? The real motivation for many advisors to steer you away from tactical investing is they are not currently in a position to sell you a product in this area. It would also be inconsistent with the sales pitch they made to you to retain your account when you were financially clobbered in 2008 and 2000–2003.

If the efficient markets and random walk theories were truly robust, one would expect to see very little active management. Funds follow performance. Interestingly, the reality is that many active managers, including hedge funds, are gaining share rather than losing share. Many of the largest mutual fund companies are mostly composed of actively managed funds. Management companies are rushing to create tactical investment products to meet rising demand.

The second issue that might slow you down in migrating toward tactical asset management is a feeling of uncertainty about how to implement a tactical investment program with confidence. What we have shown you is a proven system for knowing when to buy, what to buy, and when to sell. These are the critical decisions you need to make when investing. The following bullet points summarize the steps necessary to apply a tactical trading discipline to your portfolio.

When to Buy and Sell

- Overlay a 75-day simple moving average on a daily long-term chart of the S&P 500. When the S&P 500 crosses up through the 75-day moving average, buy. When it crosses down through the 75-day moving average, sell. Better yet ...

- Overlay a 75-day simple moving average on a daily long-term chart of the equally weighted S&P 500 represented by the Guggenheim S&P 500 Equal Weighted S&P 500 ETF (RSP). When the RSP crosses up through the 75-day moving average, buy. When it crosses down through the 75-day moving average, sell. We prefer using a nonmarket cap weighted index to judge the bullish/bearish condition of the market as it offers a broader measure of equity prices. Better yet ...

- Stay updated on the Delta Investment Management's Market Sentiment Indicator by reading *Barron's* every weekend. The MSI is published in the Market Laboratory Indicators section of the paper weekly. The MSI is based on 3,600 underlying, equally weighted equities. We use some volatility-dampening calculations to lessen the possible negative effects of whipsawing signal action. The Delta MSI can also be found on the *Barron's* website. Better yet ...

- Go to www.deltaim.com and sign up for our weekly market sentiment indicator newsletter. Every Friday, you will receive the Delta Investment Management Market Sentiment Indicator by e-mail. Better yet ...

- Sign up for *The Delta Wealth Accelerator* newsletter, which will provide ongoing market overviews and discussions of applied tactical investing.

What to Buy in a Bullish Market

- Construct a diversified portfolio of high relative strength stocks and actively manage the portfolio. Lists of high relative strength stocks can be found in the *Investor's Business Daily* newspaper or online at Investors.com.
- Buy a portfolio of high relative strength stocks by using an ETF or mutual fund.
- Buy a broad market ETF or mutual fund. You can increase expected returns increasing portfolio beta using a combination of index ETFs/mutual funds and levered index ETFs/mutual funds.

What to Buy in a Bearish Market

- Go to cash.
- For investors looking for more potential return than what is offered on cash accounts, buy short- and intermediate-term U.S. Treasury ETFs or mutual funds.
- For potentially higher returns, buy long-term U.S. Treasury bonds via an ETF or mutual fund.

This book offers a straightforward method for making consistent positive returns in stocks with a plan for avoiding major equity market losses. We provide you with an investment kit that can be used at home. Although your home kit is not as sophisticated as what is used by professionals, it will go a long way toward keeping you out of major down markets and in bullish markets. If we could find a better way to invest, we would write a book about it.

No matter what investment path you follow, your results will benefit if you do the following:

1. Use common sense.
2. Don't rely on the other guy to figure it out—understand what you are doing.
3. Be skeptical.

4. Be generally right rather than precisely wrong.
5. Invest with a plan that includes answers for:
    a. When to buy
    b. What to buy
    c. When to sell

CHAPTER EIGHTEEN

Do Enough to Make a Difference

YALE'S ENDOWMENT fund is typical of those of its peer universities, with light exposure to U.S. stocks and bonds and heavy allocation to actively managed alternatives such as hedge funds and private equity. Yale's U.S. equity allocation is just 6 percent, and its allocation to bonds and cash is even lower at 4 percent (Yale Endowment Report, September 27, 2012). Yale's allocation to private equity was 35 percent, and its allocation to absolute return strategies was 18 percent as of September 2012.

In the last 10 and 20 years, many larger university endowments easily outperformed the returns of a typical 60/40 blend of stocks and bonds and the S&P 500. For example, over the 10-year period ending June 30, 2011, Yale's endowment earned an annualized 10.1 percent return net of fees. Domestic stocks were up on an annualized basis of 3.7 percent, and domestic bonds appreciated 5.2 percent per year.

Yale's current endowment asset allocation clearly has a bearish bias toward buy-and-hold domestic equities and fixed-income assets. To ensure that the endowment has a high probability of showing meaningfully different performance than the broad stock and bond markets, it has made an outsized allocation to actively managed investment programs, including absolute return.

Rydex SGI ran a sample of returns, standard deviations, and max drawdowns for a 60/40 equity/fixed income portfolio that replaces equity by a rising amount of equitylike absolute return strategies (alternatives) for the time period December 31, 2000, through December 31, 2010. They model portfolio performance over the 10-year period with 0 percent, 5 percent, 10 percent, 20 percent, and 30 percent alternatives. What is evident is that until an investor reaches about a 20 percent allocation to alternatives, the impact on overall portfolio results is minimal. At 30 percent, the reduction in volatility and drawdowns is maximized and peak annual returns are reached.

The actual effect of replacing buy-and-hold equity investments with tactical equity strategies is somewhat more dynamic than what the Rydex SGI sample returns might suggest. If we start with a traditional 40 percent/60 percent asset allocation to bonds and equity, respectively, our pie chart would look like what is shown in Figure 18.1.

If we then replace 33 percent of the equity allocation with a tactical equity/bond strategy, the new pie chart in Figure 18.2 shows a 20 percent overall allocation to tactical.

If the tactical strategy is used to replace 33 percent of the traditional buy-and-hold equity transitions from equities to bonds in bearish markets and from bonds to equities in bullish markets, the overall portfolio automatically rebalances on the basis of current market conditions. During bearish periods, the portfolio allocation would be 60 percent bonds and 40 percent equities. During bullish

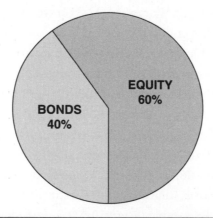

FIGURE 18.1 Portfolio with a 60 Percent/40 Percent Ratio of Equities to Bonds

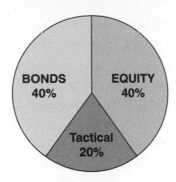

FIGURE 18.2 Portfolio with 33 Percent of the Equity Being Allocated to Tactical Equity (20 Percent of the Total Portfolio)

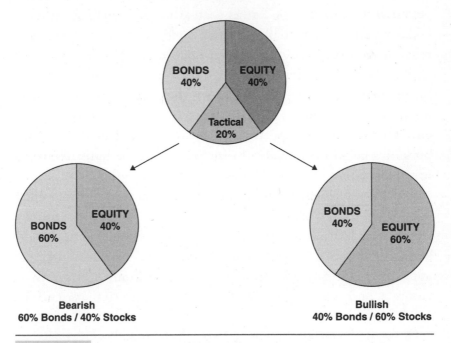

FIGURE 18.3 Dynamic Portfolio Rebalancing In Bullish and Bearish Periods

periods, the portfolio allocation would swing in the opposite direction and be 40 percent bonds and 60 percent equities (Figure 18.3).

The addition of the tactical strategy to the overall portfolio makes portfolio rebalancing proactive rather than reactive. Traditional money management advice involves rebalancing a portfolio on a periodic basis, for example, annually. The traditional rebalancing method is based on reacting to events that have already taken place. If you had carried a 40/60 split of bond and stocks through 2008, your rebalancing would have occurred after the bear market, when stocks were crushed. Now, with less capital—a smaller total pie— you would rebalance away from bonds and more toward stocks.

With a tactical strategy in the mix, a debt/equity portfolio would have been rebalanced before the market collapse and equity exposure to the bear market would have been reduced by 33 percent. The inclusion of the tactical strategy would have given an investor a bigger pie at the end of 2008. Rather than arbitrarily rebalancing at the end of a year and potentially suffering further loss, tactical strategies rebalance on the basis of an active, ongoing evaluation of market risk levels. When risk perceptions start to subside and the market begins an intermediate-term bull move, the portfolio will once again proactively rebalance to gain advantage from the improving equity environment. As the equity market recovers, gains will have been built on a larger base of assets by including tactical equity strategies in the allocation.

Investors have increasingly been using what is known as target-date or life-cycle funds to set their allocations. Target-date mutual funds automatically adjust their asset mix between stocks, bonds, and cash to derisk a portfolio as a "target date" such as retirement approaches. Derisking involves gradually transitioning investors via autopilot on a "glide path" from stocks to bonds until the target date is reached.

Research Affiliates simulated the performance of target-date funds versus a constant 50–50 stock/bond portfolio and an inverse strategy that became more aggressive over time. The target-date fund simulations underperformed both the 50–50 and the inverse risk-on strategies.

The glide path nature of target-date funds moves to a defensive posture just when the investor has enough money to make the effects of compounding highly impactful. Today, the strategy may carry even higher risk as it is migrating investors into potential negative real returns in low-yielding bonds at a time when they desperately need to build wealth to support long-duration retirement.

Investors should be wary of investment programs that make no allowance for current market conditions. Dynamic rebalancing, even yearly, on the basis of actual performance is a good idea. More frequent dynamic rebalancing that is based on forward-looking market sentiment indicators is an even better idea.

In considering what portion of your portfolio to allocate to tactical strategies, there are four important concepts to remember:

1. Take capital from the riskiest part of your portfolio to allocate to tactical strategies. Historically, stock volatility (1 standard deviation) is roughly 20 percent per year. Using volatility as the measure, stocks are likely to be the part of your portfolio that is exposed to the greatest amount of risk.

2. Redeploy capital to strategies linked to the same asset class. If you are taking money out of an equity buy-and-hold program, it should be redeployed to an equitylike alternative strategy. The objective is to retain the expected positive return profile of the most risky part of your portfolio while reducing overall portfolio risk. Reducing risk increases the chances of achieving your investment objectives.

3. Add strategies that act as a hedge during market crises. This is the purpose and objective of the tactical equity strategies described in this book.

4. Do enough to make a difference for your overall expected portfolio returns.

CHAPTER NINETEEN

Knowing If It Works: Attribution Analysis

MAYBE ONE of the simplest ways to judge whether active management works is to look at the history of Berkshire Hathaway (BRK/A). The Hathaway Manufacturing Company started in 1888 as a cotton mill. In the 1950s, Hathaway merged with Berkshire Fine Spinning Associates Inc. The combined company had 15 plants and 12,000 employees.

Because of decreasing cotton prices and foreign competition, the company closed seven plants and laid off a large number of workers by 1960. In 1962, Warren Buffett began to buy shares of the company as he thought it was undervalued. By the end of 1963, Buffett had taken ownership of 49 percent of the stock and become the company's chairman of the executive committee. He replaced old management with his management. The stock was trading at about $18 per share with only two operating mills and 2,300 employees.

Buffett transformed Berkshire Hathaway from an operating company into an investment company. In 1967, Berkshire Hathaway acquired two insurance companies. By 1985, Berkshire was entirely out of the milling business and had become a pure investment company. To participate in the fund managed by Buffett, all you had to do was buy Berkshire Hathaway Stock (BRK/A).

Buffett is an aggressive tactical manager who will watch a company for years, waiting for the perfect time to make an investment.

His specialty is buying at market lows when the competition from other bidders is virtually nonexistent. By buying when everyone else is selling, he often obtains excellent pricing and terms. One of the most attractive aspects of having Buffett run your money is that his base salary is just $100,000 per year and he does not take a fee on assets or performance, unlike almost all hedge funds.

After 1963, Berkshire Hathaway stock appreciated from $18 per share to roughly $134,000, an average return of 20 percent per year. The average return of the S&P 500 over the same time frame has been about 6.6 percent.

You might be wondering: If an active manager is truly showing material, long-term superior results, why have other competing managers not recognized the opportunity and squeezed the excess profitability out of the method? In the case of Warren Buffett, there are many investors who are essentially value investors, and some have posted excellent long-term returns. Almost none of those competitors have Buffett's mass and clout.

The very act of Berkshire Hathaway buying a stock can cause the stock to appreciate. The Berkshire Hathaway annual Letter to Shareholders is one of the most widely read documents in the financial industry, and Warren Buffett has a cult following. Corporations often want Berkshire to own their stock and will offer Berkshire special incentives to buy. This happened with a number of stock purchases Berkshire made during the credit crisis in which the firm was given special preferred dividend-paying stock and/or warrants (e.g., Goldman Sachs and Bank of America).

More generically, there are a number of important friction points in the way money is managed that allows the market to be somewhat inefficient. What *inefficient* means in this case is that consistently better than average management styles can persist for many years. Excess gains are not entirely arbitraged out of the system. Some of these friction points include the following:

1. The way financial products are sold: style boxes and fees that make money management styles somewhat rigid.
2. Clumsy portfolio allocation based on incomplete information.

3. A focus by many money management firms on asset stability rather than asset risk-adjusted return. Stable assets create a stable fee base, which is a positive for a financial company seeking to report consistent and steadily rising profits. Pursuing top-tier performance is a potential source of risk to a money management firm. Investments in fund marketing are often a better investment for the financial firm than is the pursuit of optimal portfolio performance.

4. The buy-and-hold culture built since 1970 in which investors have been told that the best strategy is to be passive.

Outperformance caused by the actions of the manager is called alpha, versus portfolio movement caused by the fluctuations of the stock market, which is called beta. If the manager's decisions are adding value, alpha is a positive number. The benchmark will always have an alpha of zero. If the manager is destroying value, alpha is a negative. The Holy Grail is investment managers who generate high positive alpha, low standard deviation, and high returns and charge low fees.

In evaluating the performance of an active investment strategy, make sure you look at the risk-adjusted returns. In other words, you may not want to place money with a manager who is able to beat the market but has much higher than market benchmark volatility. You can always amplify market returns without the manager's help by leveraging your portfolio. In this case, you are achieving outperformance simply by means of increasing beta. An attractive investment strategy has a consistent record of better than market returns with equal to or lower volatility than the benchmark market index.

In evaluating any strategy, you should ask where the excess returns (alpha) are coming from. In the case of tactical strategies, performance can come from asset selection and allocation timing decisions. If a tactical strategy is not experiencing positive absolute returns from its timing decisions, the tactical element of the strategy is not working and you might want to consider looking at other strategies. In the case of all actively managed funds, the assets selected by the manager should outperform the benchmark. Generally, outperformance is unlikely to occur if the manager owns thousands of stocks. Such broad market exposure is, at best, likely to produce broad market returns minus fees.

We have suggested that one approach to investing in equities during bullish cycles is to own a diversified portfolio of high relative strength stocks. This more concentrated portfolio offers a fair amount of diversification and an opportunity to achieve outperformance in up markets. Alternatively, for an investor who would rather not engage in individual stock trading and would like to take stock selection risk out of the equation, buying the broad market with some leverage is a satisfactory tactical investment method.

When Good Harbor is invested in equities, it achieves outperformance by applying a modest amount of leverage to its broad market exposure. In the Good Harbor case, they have increased up market (bullish) beta. Their probabilistic, multifactor model guides them to reduce equity exposure to zero in bearish markets, which causes overall portfolio beta to remain in line with the S&P 500 through the full investment cycle. Good Harbor's outperformance is mostly the result of both market timing decisions and higher beta during bullish periods.

Institutions, when analyzing fund performance, take the process several steps further by looking at up-market volatility versus down-market volatility as upside volatility is usually considered a good thing and downside volatility a negative thing. They perform "attribution analysis" to determine what is driving the outperformance.

Figure 19.1 shows how the Good Harbor team has performed in up, flat, and down markets. What the dark Good Harbor returns show is that they avoid the major down markets, are stable during flat markets, and largely participate in up markets. The returns are from May 1, 2003, through March 31, 2012.

We are seeing a rush of professional money managers coming to market with back tested tactical solutions. Take the back tested results with a grain of salt. In fact, you may not want to consider them at all. Who is going to show you poor back tested results? We promise you that the only back tested results you see will be very attractive.

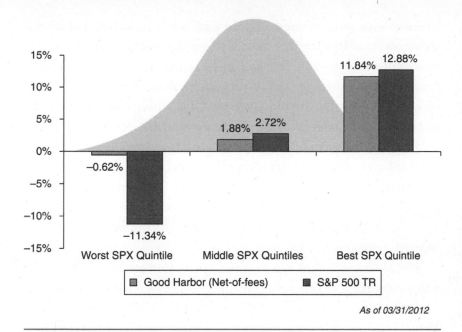

FIGURE 19.1 Good Harbor's Returns in Bullish, Flat, and Bearish Market Periods

Source: Good Harbor Financial, Bloomberg.

One of the major risks of back tested performance is how it might have been derived. A manager can back test thousands of strategy variations to find the strategy that develops the best return profile on the basis of historical market movements. There is a strong probability that if a manager tests enough possible strategies, he or she will find one that fits the data very well and produces strong results. The risk is that the strategy that best fits historical data may not perform well going forward.

The other major risk of back tested results is that the realities of trading day to day—paying brokerage charges, getting real rather than theoretical prices on large orders, and so on—create costs, particularly on small funds, that theoretical investing does not account for. It is almost always the case that back tested, theoretical performance is higher than what is achieved when these strategies go to work with real money.

In judging an investment opportunity, ask to see actual real-money results over enough time to measure how the strategy performed in a variety of market conditions. You should then ask to see an analysis of how the returns were created. If you can attribute the outperformance to actions taken by the manager rather than luck or leverage, the chances that the strategy will continue to outperform go up.

In a world where thousands of active money managers are working hard every day to outperform the market, there are going to be a few managers who show market-beating results over relatively long periods. These impressive winning streaks are to be expected. Why? Because the sample size is so large that the likelihood that there are some standouts is high.

Bill Miller with the Legg Mason Capital Management Value Trust was a classic case of this. The first rule of successful large mutual fund investing is to start the fund at a market low. Miller launched the Value Trust fund in 1982, right at the beginning of the largest bull market in history. Miller gained recognition for beating the S&P 500 for 15 years. If you invested $10,000 with Miller in 1982, it would have appreciated to $400,000 at the peak in 2006. According to Morningstar, only 26 actively managed mutual funds have beaten the market index each year over any 10-year period since 1990.

In 2007, with the S&P 500 up, Miller was down. In 2008, Legg Mason Value Trust was down 55 percent versus the S&P 500 decline of 37 percent. Miller's other fund, Legg Mason Opportunity, was down 65.5 percent that year. Investors lost interest in these funds, and in 2011 Miller stepped down.

Miller's concentrated holdings during the bull market gave him outperformance. His concentrated holdings during the bear market gave him underperformance. Miller's investing methodology essentially created high beta. There were no effective risk control measures to manage a severe market downturn. If you had invested with Miller in 2006 because of his incredible track record, you would have lost more than half your money by the end of 2008. It is really important to understand what the source of outperformance is and what kinds of risk you are exposed to when investing.

We mention the Miller experience to show the difference between high-beta investing and tactical investing involving downside risk management. Although tactical investing may underperform some of the time, it should outperform when it matters most by staying out of major down markets.

CHAPTER TWENTY

Seeing the Forest for the Fees

THE BUY-AND-HOLD cult of passive investing concentrated investors' focus almost single-mindedly on fees. Millions of investors spend most of their investment thought process on fee reduction. If you truly are a buy-and-hold investor, lowering the fees taken out of your account is about the most productive active management activity you can undertake. Your returns are likely to be whatever the market dishes out minus fees.

While you were carefully managing fees, your buy-and-hold portfolio could have suffered a 37 percent decline in 2008 if you matched the S&P 500, including dividends. You might have made virtually no real return for the 12 years ending in 2012. Your dedication to fee reduction can cause you to miss the bigger picture. A few dollars saved on fee reduction can lead to thousands of dollars lost on an inferior investment strategy. This is sometimes referred to as stepping over the dollar to pick up the penny.

The ways in which many investors manage their money ranked in order of fees are as follows:

- Self-directed investors trade their own accounts at discount brokerage firms. In the case of investors who take a long-term buy-and-hold approach, the low-fee way to follow the strategy is through low-fee index funds.

- Some investors involve an investment advisor at some level.
  Investment advisors may manage the money directly or may
  outsource all of the fund management. When advisors manage
  the money directly, it is usually in what is called a separately
  managed account. A separately managed account is an account
  held in your name at a brokerage/custodian firm managed by a
  third-party manager. Investment advisors may also use subad-
  visory agreements to manage clients' accounts or may buy what
  they believe is an attractive and appropriate allocation of mutual
  funds, ETFs, and other securities.
- High-net-worth accredited investors may invest in hedge funds.
  In the hierarchy of fund management ranked by fees, hedge
  funds rank at the top.

Being a self-directed investor may not be a bargain. Relative to
separately managed accounts, mutual fund investing can be expensive and has a substantial amount of hidden fees. Mutual funds have
fees that are explicit and fees that are hard to discern as they are
embedded in the way a fund conducts its business. All these fees add
up, and it is not uncommon to pay as much as 3 percent of one's assets
annually to own a mutual fund through an investment advisor.

Mutual Fund Explicit Fees

Expense ratio. There are costs associated with operating a mutual
   fund. These costs are deducted from your investment returns
   as a shareholder on a daily basis. It is common for the
   expense ratio fee to be about 1 percent of assets under management annually.

12B–1 fees. These fees are for marketing, distribution, and promotion of the fund. Not all funds charge 12B–1 fees. When
   they do, the annual fee level is 1 percent or less.

Loads. A load fee is a sales charge that is added to the price of a
   fund when it is purchased or sold. There are front-end and
   back-end load fees. These fees are designed to keep you in the
   fund for an extended time.

Redemption fees. Some mutual funds have no load but will charge you a redemption fee if you decide to sell the fund before a preset amount of time (e.g., 60 days). Redemption fees are designed to discourage rapid trading of the fund, which can increase fund management and transaction costs.

Transaction fees. Transaction costs are the commissions charged by your brokerage firm when you purchase or sell a mutual fund. Transaction fees are often anywhere from $0 to $50, depending on the brokerage firm and the fund you are trading.

Investment advisory fees. When you meet with financial planners or investment advisors, they usually charge you a fee. Typically, investment advisory fees range from about 0.50 percent to 2.0 percent on assets under management.

Mutual Fund Nonvisible Fees

Fund brokerage commissions. When your mutual fund manager is buying and selling stocks for the fund, the manager has to pay brokerage commissions for the trades. These commissions are paid out of the assets of the fund and are a drag on returns.

Bid/ask spreads. When you trade a stock or bond, you buy on the ask and sell on the bid. There is a spread between the bid and ask prices called the bid/ask spread. Although bid/ask spreads have become tighter with increased trading volumes and the move toward trading stocks in decimals, there is still some loss of value as a result of the spread. The impact of the spread is usually larger on stocks that rarely trade.

It is estimated that the costs to shareholders from these nonvisible fees is almost 0.8 percent annually. When you add these fees to the visible fees, it is common for mutual fund fees bought outside the guidance of an investment advisor to be about 2 percent.

Figure 20.1 shows mutual fund fees by fund type. A basis point (bp) is equal to one-hundredth of a percentage point (i.e., 100 bps is equal to 1 percent).

Expense Ratios for Selected Investment Objectives
Basis points, 2011

Investment objective	10th percentile	Median	90th percentile	Asset-weighted average	Simple average
Equity funds	78	135	220	80	144
Aggressive growth	86	140	221	92	149
Growth	73	125	209	85	137
Sector	86	146	237	86	154
Growth and income	54	115	195	50	121
Income equity	72	116	193	85	124
International equity	94	150	232	95	157
Hybrid funds	65	121	200	80	128
Bond funds	50	90	169	62	102
Taxable bond	48	93	175	63	103
Municipal bond	51	84	160	59	99
Money market funds	13	22	36	21	24

Note: Data exclude mutual funds available as investment choices in variable annuities and mutual funds that invest primarily in other mutual funds.

FIGURE 20.1 Mutual Fund Expense Ratios

Source: Investment Company Institute and Lipper.

Fees on separately managed accounts can range from 0.5 percent to 2.5 percent, with much of the business taking place between 1.25 and 2.0 percent. Although 2 percent fees may sound high, they often are not significantly different from the fees paid to actively managed mutual funds and ETFs. Separately managed accounts, if managed by the right firm, provide investors with ongoing professional assistance and support.

Hedge funds are usually limited partnerships available only to accredited high-net-worth investors. The typical hedge fund charges a fee of 2 percent on assets under management and 20 percent of all positive gains above a high-water mark. Hedge fund performance as measured by Hedge Fund Research in the HFRX for the past three and five years ending in the first quarter, 2013 is as follows:

- S&P 500 total return for three years annualized through Q1 2013, 12.7 percent; HFRX Equity Hedge Fund Index –1.1 percent
- S&P 500 total return for five years annualized through Q1 2013, 5.8 percent; HFRX Equity Hedge Fund Index –3.0 percent

A fee of 20 percent of the profits provides a strong incentive for hedge fund managers to take extraordinary risk. If their investors win, they win. If their investors lose, only the investors lose. Hedge fund management does not participate directly in the losses but takes a 20 percent cut of the gains.

In 2008, when hedge fund investors thought they were invested in funds that could show a positive return in both up and down markets, the average hedge fund declined by about 21 percent. Unable to meet redemption requests, they enacted little-noticed "gate" provisions in their management agreements that allow managers to temporarily refuse their investors' demands for cash. During 2008 and 2009, roughly 25 percent of single-strategy funds and funds of funds went out of business.

If you are considering investing in a hedge fund, make sure to ask what specifically the fund is going to hedge and how the hedge will be implemented. Ask to see the returns from just the hedge portion of the fund. Is the hedge fund adding any value by hedging? In most cases, the answer is no. If the hedge fund's hedge is not adding value to your investment, there is absolutely no reason to pay fees that are estimated to reduce hedge fund average net returns by roughly 6 percent per year.

In the separately managed account arena where many of the tactical strategies can be found, fees are relatively low and performance can be excellent. Separately managed accounts are held in the investor's name, and the investor never gives up control of the funds. Because the money is in a separate account rather than a comingled account, investors have account transparency (they receive statements and reports directly from the custodian and have 24/7 Internet access to the account) and have immediate liquidity if they want their funds right away. The money manager is given access to the account only for purposes of trading. All withdrawals from the account must be authorized by the account owner.

Fees are an important consideration in investing and potentially a significant drag on performance. Hedge fund fees make investing in this style generally unattractive. Hedge fund managers have incentives to take extraordinary risk and are likely to show underperformance over time because of the absolute magnitude of the fees. Managing your own money as a self-directed investor may be more expensive than it looks. Many funds have both explicit and hidden fees that can make self-directed investing expensive. Additionally, self-directed investors often lack the resources, experience, and discipline to show consistent outperformance over time.

If you are looking for professional help in managing your stock investments tactically, the sweet spot of active management is often in the middle ground of separately managed accounts. This is where many of the best tactical managers reside and where the fee structure does not materially erode a manager's ability to create excess return or incentivize a manager to take extraordinary risk.

The key items to think about when it comes to fees are the following:

1. Fees are an important investment consideration but are not the only consideration.
2. Many of the fees encountered in the investment world are not immediately obvious, and the total fees you are paying may be higher than what you believe to be the case.
3. When fees become too high, as in the case of hedge funds, managers' incentives may become distorted and performance may chronically lag.

4. If you are going to actively manage your money by using a tactical equity management strategy, you are likely to experience higher fees than you would with the typical buy-and-hold approach. However, it is in the tactical equity management space where the balance of performance and fees provides an excellent opportunity for wealth creation and asset protection over time.

CHAPTER TWENTY-ONE

Parting Shot

*W*IN *BY Not Losing* covers a lot of ground. Although making every effort to not lose money is a commonsense idea, the current state of the retail investment landscape makes this investment objective somewhat of an outlier. This book presents a combination of anecdotal and analytical evidence to make the case that staying out of major down equity markets should be a top priority for investors. We hope we have stimulated your interest in making loss avoidance a top priority in your personal money management.

This is the primary takeaway from *Win By Not Losing*. Participate in bullish market trends and avoid the major losing market trends. If you can execute on this simple idea, you should be a very successful investor.

It is likely you have been told that it is impossible to avoid major down equity markets and that the most prudent way to invest is to buy and hold. You certainly will not avoid major down markets if you make no attempt to do so.

The second important takeaway of *Win By Not Losing* is that there are some straightforward ways to determine when to be in and out of stocks. We measure equity market risk premium and use rising and falling broad market risk tolerance as a guide for when to invest in equities and when to avoid the market. It is not necessary to be an expert stock picker. What is more important than stock picking is picking the times to have high stock exposure and the times to limit exposure.

Tactical stock investing is unlikely to beat the broader market indexes every day. Occasional underperformance is the price of having an insurance program in place to avoid permanent, devastating losses. As we approach and enter our retirement years, this protection becomes increasingly important. Over the full investment cycle, we believe a proven tactical approach to managing a stock portfolio should outperform the traditional buy-and-hold approach. Our belief is based on experience.

The best part of following a tactical method for stock investing is that you are likely to outperform during bearish market supercycles and should also perform well in bullish market supercycles. Ultimately, tactical stock investing is about owning stocks. Stocks have provided the best long-term returns of any major asset class. Our approach to owning stocks seeks to raise the returns even higher by recognizing that gains and losses are asymmetric and that major loss avoidance is one of the most important investment actions you can take. It is Warren Buffett's first two rules of investing.

Rather than focusing on earnings as the driver of stock prices, we look at investor risk perceptions. Measuring risk perceptions by using a MAC model is relatively easy and has a long-term successful record of predicting bullish and bearish market trends. When we do own stocks, we seek to achieve high levels of up market participation by owning high relative strength stocks or by increasing portfolio beta. During bearish market periods, we preserve capital by transitioning 100 percent out of equities.

You now have a step-by-step plan to actively and dynamically manage your portfolio to compound positive returns and avoid major losses. Before investing, know when to buy, what to buy, and when to sell.

Sources

Akst, Daniel, "Knight Capital Lives and Dies by Computerized Trading," *Long Island Newsday*, August 6, 2012.

Bernard, Victor L., and Jacob K. Thomas, "Post-Earnings-Announcement Drift: Delayed Price Response or Risk Premium?" *Journal of Accounting Research*, vol. 27, Current Studies on the Information Content of Accounting Earnings, pp. 1–36, 1989.

Brown, Jeff, "Active vs. Passive: The Debate Keeps Going." *New York Times*, August 28, 2009.

Burton, Jonathan, *Revisiting the Capital Asset Pricing Model*. Reprinted with permission from *Dow Jones Asset Manager*, May/June 1998, pp. 20–28.

CBS MoneyWatch, July 16, 2010, Lessons from a Great Fund Manager's Record, Nathan Hale.

Fact File: S&P 500 Sigma Events, Jason Voss, CFA, August 27, 2012, Economics, CFA Institute.

Gilovich, Thomas, Robert Vallone, and Amos Tversky, "The Hot Hand in Basketball," *Cognitive Psychology*, vol, 17, pp. 295–314, 1985.

Harrod, R. F., *The Life of John Maynard Keynes*, 1951.

Investment Company Institute, *2012 Investment Company Fact Book*, 52d ed., http://www.icifactbook.org/index.html, http://www.ici.org/research.

Irvine, Paul J., "Jeff Vinik at Fidelity Magellan," Terry College of Business, University of Georgia, 2003.

Jones, Christopher L., *The Intelligent Portfolio: Practical Wisdom on Personal Investing from Financial Engines*. Wiley, 2008.

Keynes, John Maynard, *The General Theory of Employment, Interest and Money*, 1936.

Lo, Andrew W., and Craig MacKinlay, *A Non-Random Walk Down Wall Street.* Princeton University Press, 1999.

Mantegna, Rosario N., and H. Eugene Stanley, *An Introduction to Econophysics: Correlations and Complexity in Finance.* Cambridge, UK: Cambridge University Press, 2000.

Morningstar, http://news.morningstar.com/classroom2/course.asp?docId =145385&page=4&CN=COM/.

Russolillo, Steven, and Bill Gross, "We're Witnessing the Death of Equities," *Wall Street Journal,* July 31, 2012.

Taleb, Nassim Nicholas, *Fooled by Randomness: The Hidden Role of Change in Life and in the Markets.* Random House, 2004.

Index

About the Authors

Nicholas Atkeson is a founding partner of Delta Investment Management, LLC. Mr. Atkeson has over 17 years of industry experience. Prior to founding Delta Investment Management, Mr. Atkeson was a partner and portfolio manager of Delta Force Capital, LLC, a San Francisco based hedge fund, from 2006 to April 2009. Prior to Delta Force Capital, Mr. Atkeson was a managing director for Banc of America Securities and ThinkEquity LLC. Additionally, Mr. Atkeson helped build the institutional sales team on the West Coast for Susquehanna International Group, LLC. Mr. Atkeson is currently an editor of investment newsletters. He graduated from Haverford College, Phi Beta Kappa with a BA in economics, and from Stanford University Graduate School of Business.

Andrew Houghton is a founding partner of Delta Investment Management, LLC. Mr. Houghton has over 17 years of industry experience. Prior to founding Delta Investment Management, Mr. Houghton was a partner and portfolio manager of Delta Force Capital, a quantitative hedge fund, from 2006 until April 2009. Prior to founding and managing the hedge fund, Mr. Houghton was a managing director at ThinkEquity, and served in senior institutional sales positions at Banc of America Securities and Susquehanna International Group. Mr. Houghton is an editor of investment newsletters. He has a BA in economics from Boston University and served in the Peace Corps in Togo, West Africa.